SHARING THE SCRIPTURES

THE WORD SET FREE
VOLUME I

STUDIES IN
JUDAISM AND CHRISTIANITY

*Exploration of Issues in the
Contemporary Dialogue Between
Christians and Jews*

Editor in Chief for
Stimulus Books
Helga Croner

Editors
Lawrence Boadt, C.S.P.
Helga Croner
Rabbi Leon Klenicki
Kevin A. Lynch, C.S.P.
Dennis McManus

Sharing the Scriptures

THE WORD SET FREE
VOLUME I

Philip A. Cunningham

A STIMULUS BOOK
New York/Mahwah, N.J.

Cover design by Lynn Else
Book design by Theresa M. Sparacio

Library of Congress Cataloging-in-Publication Data

Cunningham, Philip A.
    Sharing the Scriptures / Philip A. Cunningham.
        p.   cm. — (Stimulus book)
    Includes bibliographical references.
    ISBN 0-8091-4094-2
    1. Bible. N.T.—Relation to the Old Testament. 2. Catholic Church—Relations—Judaism. 3. Judaism—Relations—Catholic Church. 4. Catholic Church—Doctrines. I. Title. II. Series
BS2387 .C86 2003
220.6—dc21

                                                            2002153724

Published by Paulist Press
997 Macarthur Boulevard
Mahwah, New Jersey 07430

www.paulistpress.com

Printed and bound in the United States of America

Contents

FOREWORD

The Stimulus Foundation came into existence in 1977, founded by Ms. Helga Croner, for the purpose of producing scholarly publications aimed at increasing mutual understanding between Christians and Jews. Over forty volumes have been published on a large number of important and often sensitive issues. These books were written by some of the most distinguished scholars in the Jewish and Christian communities. They have found a wide and receptive audience. Paulist Press has been honored to be an active partner in this significant undertaking.

With the presentation of The Word Set Free, the Stimulus Foundation offers a new and somewhat different series. It deals in practical ways with the presentation of Judaism in the Bible, especially the books of the New Testament. The series is written by highly qualified scholars but at a very popular level. It is intended for both Christian leaders—preachers, homiletic professors, teachers, and religious educators—and for Christian and Jewish groups that wish to meet together in dialogue. Each book in the series reveals both the appreciation of Judaism by the early Christian community and how its simultaneous disparagement of Judaism set the stage for so much of the anti-Semitism in the centuries that followed.

I wish to express the gratitude of the Stimulus Board to Rabbi Leon Klenicki and Mr. Dennis McManus for their diligent and dedicated editorial work on this project. We hope The Word Set Free will make a significant contribution to improved Jewish and Christian understanding.

Kevin A. Lynch, C.S.P.
President, The Stimulus Foundation

PREFACE

A. Historical Overview: A Renewal in the Church's Appreciation of the "Old Testament"

The practice in both the Roman and common lectionaries of excerpting the sacred texts of ancient Israel and juxtaposing them with portions of the Christian gospels raises a number of complex issues. Among them are the revelatory worth of Israel's scriptures, the methods of interpretation that should govern the interplay between different texts, the spiritual legitimacy of Judaism today, Christian self-understanding, and the relationship between Judaism and Christianity.

Since the days of the apostles, Christians have consulted Israel's ancient sacred writings in order to help comprehend their experiences of the Crucified and Raised One. This, of course, is not surprising because, as Pope John Paul II has noted, "it is impossible fully to express the mystery of Christ without reference to [them]."[1] Moreover, since Jesus himself "came humanly to know these texts; he nourished his mind and heart with them, using them in prayer and as an inspiration for his actions,"[2] it is only logical that his earliest followers, all of whom were also Jewish, would do the same.

In the second through fourth centuries, however, this natural reliance on Israel's sacred writings assumed a different tone because of the church's overwhelmingly Gentile membership and because of its marginal social status in the Roman Empire in comparison with a vibrant and respected Judaism. In defending themselves against the charges of Roman critics that Christianity was a heretical distortion of Judaism, church leaders faced the difficult task of claiming that they understood Jewish texts better than Jews did. It was an especially

This preface was studied and discussed at the April 20, 2001 meeting of the Christian Scholars Group of the Institute for Christian and Jewish Studies in Baltimore. I am grateful for the lively conversation that helped to refine a number of points in the eassy.

vexing challenge to explain the apparently contradictory Christian beliefs that Israel's scriptures, including the "Law of Moses," were indeed inspired by God, but that the church was not obligated to follow that Law.[3]

The strategies devised to meet these problems set the pattern of Christian approaches to the Torah, the Prophets, and the Writings for more than a millennium. One solution that was rejected was that of Marcion. He claimed that the God of Jesus had not inspired Israel's scriptures, but rather that an evil deity was their source. This idea was deemed heretical by the vast majority of church leaders, most of whom sought to explain the Christian understanding of what they called the "Old Testament" along the lines conveniently summarized here by Augustine of Hippo:

> [The Jewish] people, then, received the Law written by the finger of God on tablets which were, it is true, of stone, to typify the hardness of their hearts because they were not to fulfill the Law.... Therefore, they were burdened down with many visible ordinances that thereby they might be weighed down as beneath a yoke of bondage, in matters of observances in foods, in sacrifices of animals, and in other things innumerable; all these things, nevertheless, were tokens of spiritual things relating to the Lord Jesus Christ and to the Church. These were then understood [spiritually] by a few holy men so as to bear the fruit of salvation, and were observed in accordance with the fitness of the time, but by the multitude of carnal men they were observed only, not understood.[4]

> If, moreover, all divine Scripture that was written before was written to foretell the coming of the Lord...therefore, in the Old Testament the New

is concealed, and in the New the Old is revealed. In keeping with that concealment, carnal men, understanding only carnally, both then were, and now are, made subject to fear of punishment. But in keeping with this revelation spiritual men, understanding spiritually...are made free by the bestowal of love.[5]

As Augustine's remarks show, the "Old Testament" was understood by the church fathers to be merely preparatory for the coming of Christ and the church. To perceive this reality, the "Old Testament" had to be read in a spiritual sense, that is, as symbolizing or foreshadowing Christ and the church. Jews, it was supposed, read things only in a carnal or literal sense and so failed to understand the transitory nature of their religious traditions in general and of the Mosaic Law in particular. Those who read the ancient texts "spiritually" perceived that the Jewish religion was an onerous way of life based on fear and that it had always been destined by God for replacement by Christianity, the religion of love.

Thus, in patristic times a negative assessment of Judaism became entangled with Christian "Old Testament" reading habits. Known today as *supersessionism*, this replacement theology asserted that Christianity had superseded Judaism, that the "New Testament" had completed the "Old," and that the wandering homelessness of unbelieving Jews was proof of this. A corresponding caricature of Judaism as oppressive, legalistic, and moribund emerged, and dominated Christian thought until only recently.

In medieval times Christians were certainly aware of different "senses" in which the Bible could be read. One rhyme that circulated widely described four interpretive methods: literal, allegorical (which foreshadowed Christ or the church), ethical, and eschatological (or anagogic, which pointed to the ultimate future):

> The letter shows us what God and our fathers did;
> The allegory shows us where our faith is hid;
> The moral meaning gives us rules of our daily life;
> The analogy shows us where we end our strife.[6]

While there were debates as to which of these senses was the most important, there is no evidence that the medieval appreciation of a variety of approaches prompted any sustained reading of the "Old Testament" that did not presuppose that Israel's covenanted status had been supplanted by the Church.

Two developments have undercut typical supersessionist attitudes toward the "Old Testament." First, the widespread adoption of scientific, critical methods of reading the Bible led to the understanding that the scriptures have intrinsic meanings rooted in their historical and literary contexts. They have inherent value irrespective of later traditions of interpretation. With this perspective, some Christians began to read the first part of their Bible within its own frames of reference instead of immediately leaping to christological construals. Such historical-critical or literary-critical readings of ancient Israel's scriptures are partly a reassertion of the priority of the literal sense. This sense, it was increasingly felt, should not be lost in subsequent applications of the biblical texts, including those applications that occur within the Christian gospels.

For example, in Hosea 11:1–4, the prophet, speaking on behalf of God, depicts Israel's history in this way:

> **11** When Israel was a child, I loved him,
>   　　and out of Egypt I called my son.
> 　² The more I called them,
>   　　the more they went from me;
>   　they kept sacrificing to the Baals,
>   　　and offering incense to idols.

[3] Yet it was I who taught Ephraim to walk,
    I took them up in my arms;
        but they did not know that I healed them.
[4] I led them with cords of human kindness,
        with bands of love.
    I was to them like those
        who lift infants to their cheeks.
        I bent down to them and fed them.

Plainly, Hosea intends to portray the God of Israel as a loving caretaker and parent, whose devotion to Israel from its birth during the Exodus up to the time of Hosea has not been reciprocated. This meaning is not abrogated by the later application of "Out of Egypt I have called my son" in Matthew 2:15 to the tale of the infant Jesus being hidden in Egypt from the murderous plots of Herod the Great. A supersessionist reading of this Hosea text would see it only as prefiguring the story of Jesus, including perhaps a lack of recognition of Jesus as Israel's healer. A critical reading deems as crucially important Hosea's perceptions of God's intimate love for Israel in his own eighth-century B.C.E. context.[7] It also identifies and esteems Matthew's conviction that the story of Israel is retold and embodied in the story of Jesus. In the latter approach the spiritual legitimacy of Israel's experience is necessary in order for Matthew's portrayal of Jesus to be sensible.

The second twentieth-century development that undermined prior supersessionist habits was the reexamination of Christian teachings begun by many churches in the aftermath of the *Shoah*. A milestone in this reappraisal was the 1965 promulgation by the Second Vatican Council of the Roman Catholic Church of a *Declaration on the Relationship of the Church to Non-Christian Religions*, known by its Latin title of *Nostra Aetate*. Chapter 4 of this document repudiated the foundational principle of supersessionism by stating that "the

Jews remain very dear to God" and by quite explicitly instructing that "the Jews should not be spoken of as rejected or
accursed as if this followed from holy scripture. Consequently,
all must take care, lest in catechizing or in preaching the word
of God, they teach anything which is not in accord with the
truth of the Gospel message or the spirit of Christ."[8] Many
other Christian communities produced similar declarations.
The Presbyterian Church USA, for instance, stated: "To this
day, the church's worship, preaching, and teaching often lend
themselves, at times unwittingly, to a perpetuation of the
'teaching of contempt.'…The church's attitudes must be
reviewed and changed as necessary, so that they never again
fuel the fires of hatred."[9]

Some of the official documents produced by Christian
churches after the *Shoah* specifically considered the subject
of the Christian use of the "Old Testament."[10] Of particular
importance is the Vatican's 1985 "Notes on the Correct Way
to Present the Jews and Judaism in Preaching and Catechesis
in the Roman Catholic Church." After observing that Christians can profit from Jewish readings of the ancient Israelite
texts, the document went on to say that christological readings only manifest "the unfathomable riches of the Old Testament, its inexhaustible content and the mystery of which it
is full, and should not lead us to forget that it retains its own
value as Revelation that the New Testament often does no
more than resume."[11]

This idea was further developed by the U.S. Catholic
Bishops' Committee on the Liturgy, which advised preachers
in 1988 that "the Hebrew Scriptures are the word of God
and have validity and dignity in and of themselves" and that,
therefore, they should "avoid approaches that reduce them
to a propaedeutic or background for the New Testament."[12]

The common recognition of both biblical criticism and
the renewal in Jewish and Christian relations that "the same

biblical text, therefore, can have more than one valid hermeneutical interpretation, ranging from its original historical context and intent to traditional Christological applications"[13] is not precisely new. It recalls the four senses of the medieval rhyme. The difference between recent and earlier Christian readings of Israel's ancient texts is the absence today of the supersessionist presuppositions that effectively reduced those texts to only one really salvifically relevant meaning. These scriptures are now viewed as manifestations of Israel's ongoing covenantal life with the God who saves both in the ancient past and in the world of today.

Another important distinction between supersessionist and post-supersessionist readings should be stressed here. It is one thing to read the scriptures of ancient Israel, as the apostles did, to understand Jesus Christ more insightfully. It is another thing to demean the spiritual worth of those texts by valuing *only* christological construals of them. The first practice simply respects the truth that Jesus was "an authentic son of Israel, deeply rooted in his own people's long history."[14] The second inevitably leads, as history has shown, to a supersessionist devaluation of Judaism and its scriptures.

Thus, it is perfectly appropriate for the lectionary to pair readings from the gospels with passages from the traditions of Israel for homiletic use at church worship: Christians can thereby come to a deeper relationship with the God of Israel whom Christ embodies and reveals. But there is the danger that the lectionary's pairings could limit an appreciation of the "inexhaustible wealth" of the "Old Testament" readings to only their christological applications and thereby encourage the anti-Jewish attitudes that have characterized the church's supersessionist history.

Preaching and teaching based on the lectionary, then, are especially obligated to promote an awareness of the divinely inspired and multidimensional richness of the scriptures of an ancient people whose descendants remain a living community of faith today. The rest of this book will suggest ways to accomplish this important task. In considering them, readers may come to the conclusion that the title of this series, The Word Set Free, is particularly relevant for this volume's subject—the use of the scriptures of ancient Israel in the lectionary.

B. New Names for a New Relationship

The growing awareness that supersessionist attitudes have habitually accompanied Christian readings of the sacred writings of ancient Israel has recently engendered steady conversation about what language is most fitting to use for the two parts of the church's Bible.[15] The traditional terms "Old Testament" and "New Testament" are unsettling to those who fear they promote the now repudiated theology that the church has superseded Judaism. They are also concerned that "Old" is too easily viewed as outmoded or obsolete, particularly in youth-oriented Western society in which computer chips are out-of-date upon purchase. New Testament texts that describe the first covenant as "obsolete and growing old, soon to disappear" (Heb 8:13) or portray the old covenant as concealed by a veil that is "set aside only in Christ" (2 Cor 3:14) exacerbate these worries.[16] The conversation has been under way in many Christian denominations and has included Jewish participants.

Sensitivity to the issue is evident in some recent Christian texts. In a speech to Australian Jews, for example, Pope John Paul II noted, "For the Jewish people themselves, Catholics should have not only respect but also great fraternal love, for it is the teaching of both the Hebrew Scriptures and the Christian Scriptures that the Jews are beloved of God, who has called them with an irrevocable calling."[17] Likewise, although the Vatican Commission for Religious Relations with the Jews retained the traditional Old/New Testament terms in its 1985 "Notes," it felt it necessary to explain that "'old' does not mean 'out of date' or 'outworn'" and that it was going to emphasize "the *permanent* value of the Old Testament as a source of Christian revelation."[18] In a similar vein, the Synod of the Evangelical Church of the Rhineland noted in a 1980 statement:

> Throughout the centuries the word "new" has been used in biblical exegesis against the Jewish people: the new covenant was understood in contrast to the old covenant, the new people of God as a replacement of the old people of God. This disrespect to the permanent election of the Jewish people and its condemnation to non-existence marked Christian theology, the preaching and work of the church again and again right to the present day.[19]

Ecclesial and academic individuals or groups have experimented with many alternatives. Among the terms used instead of Old Testament are "Prior Testament,"[20] "Former Covenant,"[21] "Prime Testament,"[22] "Common Testament,"[23] "First Testament,"[24] and "Hebrew Scriptures,"[25] the last two being the most popular. New Testament is not replaced as often as Old Testament, but substitutes for it include "Apostolic Writings,"[26] "Christian Testament,"[27] and "Second Testament."[28]

None of these alternatives has been universally adopted, and serious criticisms have been leveled against some of them. First/Second Testament and Hebrew/Christian scriptures are both vulnerable to the charge that they inadequately express the canonical continuity of the entire Christian Bible: they can sound like unconnected collections and so smack of the heresy of Marcion. Hebrew scriptures is also faulted because it implies that the Christian Old Testament and the Jewish *Tanakh* (the Hebrew acronym of the three parts of the Jewish scriptures) are identical, even though they have different books (not all written in Hebrew) and different arrangements of those books.[29] The lack of agreement on the topic has been brought to the attention of the general public in an essay in *The New York Times Magazine* that surveys the issues involved.[30]

The fact that the conversation has arisen because of the modern church's rejection of supersessionism suggests that the question is primarily a theological one. "Old Testament" accurately conveyed the patristic church's supersessionist understanding of the traditions and texts of Judaism. Current discomfort with the term appears because it does not accord with our new theological perspectives about God's eternal covenant with Israel. Therefore, terminological issues will not be resolved solely on the basis of exegetical or linguistic considerations. Rather, Christianity's emerging, though still immature, post-supersessionist, positive theology of Judaism must be the foundation upon which non-supersessionist and affirmative terms for the Testaments can be devised.

The extensive documentary tradition on Jewish and Christian relations already composed by the ecclesial authorities of a variety of denominations offers some important theological cues. This section will sketch these theological principles and suggest a consequent terminology.

1. The Covenant Between God and Israel Endures.

Beginning with *Nostra Aetate* in 1965 and repeated ever more forcefully in subsequent documents, many Christian denominations have taught that the Christian covenant with God in Christ has not ended the earlier covenantal life between God and the people of Israel. Many Christian communities would agree with the words of the United Church of Christ, USA, that "God's covenant with the Jewish people has not been rescinded or abrogated by God, but remains in full force."[31]

2. In Their Ongoing Covenant with God, Jews Have Developed a Rich Spiritual History and Tradition from Which Christians Should Learn.

Besides urging that Christians must "strive to learn by what essential traits the Jews define themselves in the light of their own religious experience,"[32] several ecclesial instructions have praised the richness of the Jewish heritage down to the present:

> The history of Israel did not end in 70 A.D....It continued, especially in a numerous Diaspora which allowed Israel to carry on to the whole world a witness—often heroic—of its fidelity to the one God and to "exalt him in the presence of all the living" (Tb. 13:4)....We must remind ourselves how the permanence of Israel is accompanied by a continuous spiritual fecundity in the rabbinical period, in the Middle Ages, and in modern times, taking its start from a patrimony which we long shared.[33]

Therefore, as John Paul II has observed, Christians can learn from "that heritage, but also [from] the faith and religious life of the Jewish people as professed and lived now as well."[34] This sentiment echoed the observation of the Executive Committee of the World Council of Churches that "in dialogue with Jews many Christians come to a more profound appreciation of the Exodus hope of liberation, and pray and work for the coming of righteousness and peace on earth."[35] Thus, the U.S. Catholic Bishops' Committee on the Liturgy further advised preachers to "be free to draw on Jewish sources (rabbinic, medieval, modern) in expounding the meaning of the Hebrew Scriptures and the apostolic writings."[36]

3. Christians Should Understand That the "Old Testament" Has More Than One Valid Interpretation and That They Can Benefit from Jewish Readings of It.

Several recent documents have urged Christians "to acquire a better understanding of whatever in the Old Testament retains its own perpetual value, since that has not been canceled by the later interpretation of the New Testament."[37] Even though "Christian identity and Jewish identity should be carefully distinguished in their respective reading of the Bible...this detracts nothing from the value of the Old Testament in the Church and does nothing to hinder Christians from profiting discerningly from the traditions of Jewish reading."[38] This is because the "Old Testament" possesses an "inexhaustible content" and "unfathomable riches" and "retains its own value as revelation that the New Testament often does no more than resume."[39]

4. Modern Jews and Christians Share a Common Heritage and, by God's Will, the Two Traditions Are Intrinsically Connected.

Many ecclesial instructions have stressed the common roots of Jews and Christians. The Texas Conference of Churches put it this way in 1982:

> We confess thankfully the Scriptures of the Jewish people, the Old Testament of our Bible, to be the common foundation for the faith and work of Jews and Christians. By referring to the Hebrew Scriptures as the "Old Testament" it is not our intention to imply that these Scriptures are not timelessly new for both Jew and Christian today.[40]

This recognition leads to major educational conse-
quences, as the 1985 Vatican "Notes" declared:

> Because of the unique relations that exist between
> Christianity and Judaism—"linked together at the
> very level of their identity" (John Paul II, 6th
> March, 1982)—relations "founded on the design of
> the God of the Covenant" (ibid.), the Jews and
> Judaism should not occupy an occasional and mar-
> ginal place in catechesis: their presence there is
> essential and should be organically integrated.[41]

As this quotation shows, the link between the two living
faith traditions has been an important topic for John Paul II.
This is made even clearer by his comments in the chief synagogue in Rome:

> The Church of Christ discovers her "bond" with
> Judaism by "searching into her own mystery" (cf.
> *Nostra Aetate*). The Jewish religion is not "extrin-
> sic" to us, but in a certain way is "intrinsic" to our
> own religion. With Judaism therefore we have a
> relationship which we do not have with any other
> religion. You are our dearly beloved brothers and,
> in a certain way, it could be said that you are our
> elder brothers.[42]

To sum up: Given the fact that the Christian biblical canon
is an expression of Christian theology and self-definition, it is
essential that our testamental terminology reflect current
Christian post-supersessionist theology as abstracted in the four
principles described above.

On this basis, it seems plain that the terms Old Testa-
ment/New Testament, Prior Testament, and Former Testament are all inadequate in the church's new context vis-à-vis
Judaism. None of them connotes that Judaism is a vibrant and

continuing religious tradition; indeed, they can suggest the opposite. To a lesser extent this is also true of First/Second Testament and Hebrew/Christian scriptures, but their more significant problem is that they don't convey that these texts are an organic component of the Christian scriptural heritage as well. In other words, the Hebrew scriptures are also Christians' scriptures. Common Testament avoids all of these pitfalls, but it seems focused on past origins and does little to express current Christian convictions about the intrinsic spiritual bonds between living Judaism and Christianity today. It also can connote the mundane or the ordinary.

Ideally, there should be terms that articulate and convey the new theological understanding about Jewish and Christian relations each and every time that they are used. I propose that the language of "Shared Testament" reflects the modern church's stance toward Jews and Judaism. These are texts that are shared in different ways by two living faith communities. Using a fortunate nuance from the Latin *testamentum*, they are also texts that testify to Judaism's and Christianity's shared spiritual roots in ancient Hebrew spirituality. Both traditions are living heirs of the Hebrew legacy, even if we arrange and interpret the texts differently and include a few different works.

As a "testament," Shared Testament also recognizes the canonical value of these texts as part of the Christian Bible, a weakness in the "Hebrew scriptures" approach. Furthermore, Shared Testament plainly entertains no possibility that the "Old" has been superseded by the "New."

For Christians, there is another benefit: Shared Testament says that there is a living spiritual tradition apart from the church that also sees these texts as canonical. It suggests that there are other legitimate, even if non-Christian, ways to read these texts. In other words, "Shared" Testament affirms all the recent, positive church understandings about which "Old" Testament is ambiguous at best.

The "Christian Testament," then, is understood as those texts that are held to be scriptural only by Christian communities. They are the inspired testimony or legacy of the apostolic generations of the church. Christian Testament thus expresses these texts' canonical status better than "Apostolic Writings." It also avoids the supersessionist potentials of the traditional "New" Testament.

Jews are not being asked here to adopt these terms for their own use. For Jews to speak of their *Tanakh* as also being the "Shared Testament" in interfaith settings might be thought of as fitting, but such usage could be interpreted as more than a historical acknowledgment of common roots. It might be construed as a theological statement about a divine sanctioning of Christianity, or of Jews and Christians as covenantal partners in the world. The acceptability for Jews of such ideas would have to be determined by Jews themselves. However, the use of Shared Testament and Christian Testament by *Christians* is essentially a matter of articulating a renewed Christian theology. Provided that caricatures or hostility are not being promoted, this Christian endeavor for adequate Christian speech is not something in which Jews play a direct role.

The expression "Shared Testament" has its drawbacks, too. If people understand *testament* according to its origins in the Greek word for "covenant," then a shared covenant and a Christian covenant would be confusing theology.[43] Of course, the traditional language of "Old Covenant" and "New Covenant" is also problematic theologically because of its supersessionist potential.[44] This objection can be readily addressed through preaching and education that reinforces the colloquial understanding of "testament" as "legacy or witness."

Some may find "shared" to be too saccharine or syrupy. Given the need for a short, concise phrase that rightly reflects the church's new theological awareness and that also bears some resemblance to traditional usage, however, other alternatives are hard to find.

It may also be the case that the sheer inertia of the long use of "Old Testament" will inhibit change. Such a shift from ancient practice is not an easy thing to undertake. On the other hand, shouldn't Christian terms accurately express Christian theology? Since the church has already made enormous strides in reforming, and indeed reversing, its stance toward the Jewish community, perhaps there is a recent precedent even for a major and defining shift in speech. This sort of terminology change, in which the Christian Bible is understood to contain two parts— the Shared Testament and the Christian Testament—would be consistent with the Spirit-prompted renewal of Christian attitudes toward Jews and, indeed, is probably demanded by it. Shouldn't Augustine's oft-quoted, but essentially supersessionist statement about the Testaments be reworded to reflect our reformed theology?: "In the Shared Testament, the rabbinic texts and the Christian Testament find their perpetual foundations; in the Christian Testament, the Shared Testament is intensely read anew in Christ."

I also argue that any testamental terminology should be used consistently. It would not be faithful to post-supersessionist theology, for example, for Christians to talk about the Shared Testament in interfaith settings and then revert to Old Testament at their own liturgies or in the Roman or common lectionaries. Moreover, for a Christian congregation to hear a reading introduced as "Our Shared Testament reading today is from the Book of Genesis..." could do more to impart post-supersessionist attitudes than all the documents produced by the diverse churches after the *Shoah*, as impressive as that body of statements is. In an effort to express the church's renewed appreciation for Judaism and as an experiment in alternative usage, from this point on this volume will use the terms "Shared Testament" and "Christian Testament." Indeed, the purpose of this volume is to help preachers and teachers to interpret the lectionary excerpts of the texts of ancient Israel as a Shared Testament for their congregations and pupils. To summarize the reasons for this terminology, Shared Testament and Christian Testament:

1. use short, recognizable words that require little explanation in pastoral settings;
2. convey the scriptural authority of both collections for Christians;
3. do not imply supersessionism;
4. reflect the historical reality that both rabbinic Judaism and Christianity are descendants of ancient Hebrew spirituality;
5. suggest that two living faith communities are mysteriously linked in God's plan and can learn from one another; and
6. best articulate the church's new theological perspectives on Jews and Judaism.

It is to be hoped that this attempt to name the church's new theological awareness about Jews, Judaism, and the eternal, inspired, and multifaceted character of the scriptures of ancient Israel will point to workable approaches for the future.

C. Biblical Principles for Interpreting the Shared Testament

Returning to the danger that the lectionary's excerpting of the Shared Testament can inadvertently promote anti-Jewish attitudes, helpful perspectives are offered by contemporary principles of critical biblical interpretation. Guidelines for using the lectionary's Shared Testament selections in affirming and non-supersessionist ways can be outlined in the following four points.

1. Efforts Must Be Made to Determine the Intended Meanings of a Scriptural Text Within Its Own Frames of Reference. This Requires an Understanding of the Historical Situations and Literary Conventions of the Sacred Writers.

An important articulation of the need to read biblical passages in their historical contexts was offered by the Second Vatican Council: "However, since God speaks in sacred Scripture through people in human fashion, the interpreter of sacred Scripture, in order to see clearly what God wanted to communicate to us, should carefully investigate what meaning the sacred writer really intended, and what God wanted to manifest by means of their words."[45] The concept was expressed in a more sophisticated way in a later instruction of the Pontifical Biblical Commission. It stated that the Roman Catholic community:

> recognizes that one of the aspects of biblical texts is that they are the work of human authors, who employed both their own capacities for expression and the means which their age and social context put at their disposal. Consequently Catholic exegesis freely makes use of the scientific methods and approaches which allow a better grasp of the meaning of texts in their linguistic, literary, sociocultural, religious and historical contexts, while explaining them as well through studying their sources and attending to the personality of each author.[46]

The second quotation recognizes that it is impossible simply to enter the mind and heart of an ancient author and so know fully what meanings were precisely intended. Nonetheless, the Biblical Commission asserts that the effort to comprehend a text in its historical and literary settings is an essential first step in critical biblical interpretation.

As Sandra Schneiders has expressed it, a written text has an "ideal meaning," a mental structure arising from a dialectic between the sense (what the text claims grammatically and syntactically) and the reference (the veracity or reality of its claim) of the text.[47] In this conception, the work of the biblical critic in establishing the "ideal meaning" (or perhaps "intended meaning") of the text provides an objective pole of interpretation that must be realized in all subsequent applications or explications of the text.[48] Even though twenty-first-century readers cannot make absolute claims about what an author intended to say in a written text, it is possible through literary and historical analyses to determine the overall parameters of what a text seeks to convey.

This inevitably leads to a conclusion that was made earlier. When considering an excerpt from the Shared Testament, one must keep in mind that the ideal meaning put in writing by the Hebrew or Jewish author "retains its own perpetual value…[which] has not been canceled by the later interpretation of the New [Christian] Testament."[49] Indeed, the "inexhaustible content" of the Shared Testament is such that "it retains its own value as revelation that the New [Christian] Testament often does no more than resume."[50]

When teaching or preaching from the lectionary, then, the meaning intended by the Shared Testament text within its own particular historical and social and literary setting must be considered first. Failure to do so would be to dismiss the inspired experiences and insights of the author who inscribed the text and, therefore, to deny that God is meaningfully encountered in the midst of the concrete historical circumstances of real human beings.

2. As the Various Biblical Books Came into Being, Their Authors Reread and Reinterpreted Older Books and So Developed New Meanings That Were Not Originally Present.

This point is absolutely crucial in devising a workable pastoral approach that respects the complex intertextual relations between the Shared and Christian Testaments. In the words of the Pontifical Biblical Commission: "Later biblical writings often depend upon earlier ones. These more recent writings allude to older ones, [and] create 'rereadings' which develop new aspects of meaning, sometimes quite different from the original sense."[51] To illustrate this point, the commission offered several examples from the Shared Testament. For instance, Jeremiah's reference to Judah's punishment by the Babylonians for seventy years (Jer 25:11–12; 29:10) is considered to have been satisfied in the past by the author of Chronicles (2 Chr 25:20–23) but is thought by the writer of Daniel 9:24–27 to find its true meaning in the struggle with Antiochus IV in his own era.[52]

This same rereading process was at work in the composition of the Christian Testament. The Jewish apostles and evangelists made use of the Shared Testament for a number of reasons. First, the scriptures of ancient Israel helped them to understand the meaning and significance of their experiences of the Crucified and Raised One. Second, they drew upon the motifs and perspectives of the Torah, the Prophets, and the Writings as they sought to evangelize others in the good news of Christ. Third, they also argued their interpretation of the sacred texts with other Jews who did not read them with their presuppositions about the centrality of Christ.

For example, Psalm 22 is the personal lament of an individual beset by an extreme illness or some other affliction whose enemies are pouncing upon his weaknesses and despoiling him of his possessions. The psalmist moves from a sense of despair and complaint to a declaration of praise of the sovereignty of God. Because of similarities with the laments of Jeremiah (see Jer 20:7–18), some have seen his influence in the present shape of the song. There is no evidence that Second Temple period Jews understood this psalm in any predictive way, and the speaker was typically understood as the symbol of the righteous sufferer who represented the experience of all Israel.

Yet probably all Christians think of Jesus when this psalm is heard. From the opening cry—"My God, my God, why have you abandoned me?"—to the dividing up of the clothes of the sufferer to the reference to the "piercing" of hands and feet (although the meaning of the Hebrew word is very unclear and might mean "withered" or "picked clean"), Christians reflexively recall Jesus' death by crucifixion. This is partly because the evangelists, beginning with Mark, all used Psalm 22 to shape their descriptions of the execution of Jesus. The earliest Christians, trying to come to grips with the horrible death of a noble and holy person, and the amazement of his unforeseen resurrection, found insight in Psalm 22's pattern of the suffering, just man who praises God's vindication of him. They read the psalm christologically and patterned their portrayals of his death on elements in it. Unlike Jews, who did not share their resurrection experience, they read Psalm 22 messianically as reflective of the life, death, and divine vindication of God's Anointed One.[53]

Such a process of rereading earlier scriptures is the reason why it is perfectly appropriate for the lectionary to juxtapose Shared Testament and Christian Testament passages.

Listeners or students can see how the evangelists drew on Israel's story as they came to grips with their overwhelming experience of Jesus. Therefore, the second principle in preaching or teaching the Shared Testament from the lectionary is to indicate how the gospel resonates with Israel's experience in the Shared Testament reading. The verb *resonate* is chosen with care. The gospel passage must not be proclaimed as emptying or terminating the revelatory worth of the Shared Testament. Nor should the Shared Testament passage be reduced to a mere prediction that the gospel reading effectuates. Rather, the authentic insights into God's dealings with humanity contained in the Shared Testament must be shown to be reaffirmed, echoed, and intensely recurring in the ministry, death, and ongoing resurrected life of Jesus. How this might work in practice will be illustrated in the examples that follow.

3. Interpreting the Bible Today Involves a Dialogue Between the Faith Experiences of the Biblical Writers and Those of the Church Today.

Beyond seeking to grasp the meaning that a biblical text originally was meant to have and the meanings that it generated over the centuries is the need to *actualize* the text or to relate the text to our world of today. Whether conscious of it or not, we read the scriptures today with our own histories, philosophical conceptions, issues, and questions. This shapes our reading of the texts and permits us to perceive meanings or implications that previous generations of readers did not share. As the Pontifical Biblical Commission expressed it in 1993:

> Sacred Scripture is in dialogue with communities of believers: It has come from their traditions of faith....Dialogue with Scripture in its entirety,

which means dialogue with the understanding of
the faith prevailing in earlier times, must be
matched by a dialogue with the generation of
today. Such dialogue will mean establishing a
relationship of continuity. It will also involve
acknowledging differences. Hence, the interpretation of Scripture involves a work of sifting and
setting aside; it stands in continuity with earlier
exegetical traditions, many elements of which it
preserves and makes its own; but in other matters
it will go its own way, seeking to make further
progress.[54]

This very rich statement witnesses to the enormous
dynamism of biblical interpretation. To read the Bible fully is
to enter into a living encounter with the God who was in relationship with our ancestors in faith and who is in relationship
with us today. Sometimes the texts of our forebears will be
uncomfortably challenging for us and we will be found wanting. The Bible's constant concern for the plight of the poor,
for instance, can unsettle those living in complacent affluence.
At other times insights produced during the history subsequent to the Bible's composition will enable modern readers to
find the text itself wanting, for example, in rejecting the Bible's
tacit acceptance of slavery.

A relevant point about actualizing biblical texts today
needs to be made here. There are many Shared Testament and
Christian Testament texts that are eschatological in nature.
This means that they refer to the end-times, to the ultimate
destiny of all creation when the peace and justice willed by
God prevail everywhere. A good example of an eschatological
text is Isaiah 2:2–4:

In the days to come the mountain of the Lord's
house shall be established as the highest of the

mountains, and shall be raised above the hills; many peoples shall come and say, "Come, let us go up to the mountain of the Lord, to the house of the God of Jacob; that he may teach us his ways and that we may walk in his paths." For out of Zion shall go forth instruction, and the word of the Lord from Jerusalem. He shall judge between the nations, and shall arbitrate for many peoples; they shall beat their swords into plowshares and their spears into pruning hooks; nation shall not lift up the sword against nation, neither shall they learn war anymore.

This eschatological passage clearly looks toward a day that has not yet arrived—a day of universal peace when all the earth walks in God's ways.

When over the centuries some of these eschatological texts were read by Christians thinking about Jesus, they actualized them as having been fulfilled in him. In some cases this required a spiritualizing or major reinterpretation of the text, but in other cases, such as Isaiah's hope that one day "the eyes of the blind will be opened, and the ears of the deaf unstopped" (Isa 35:5), the association with Jesus was rather straightforward.

Some recent ecclesial documents stress that the eschaton has not yet arrived in its fullness. The lion does not yet lie down with the lamb, and nations still prepare for war. This idea has perhaps been most fully expressed by the U.S. Bishops' Committee on the Liturgy, which noted that such texts

are not merely temporal predictions but profound expressions of eschatological hope....This hope includes trust in what is promised but not yet seen. While the biblical prophecies of an age of universal shalom are "fulfilled" (i.e., irreversibly inaugurated) in Christ's coming, that fulfillment is not yet completely worked out in each person's life or in the world at large....It is the mission of the church, as also that of the Jewish people, to proclaim and to work to prepare the world for the full flowering of God's Reign, which is, but is "not yet."[55]

This provides a guiding principle when seeking to actualize eschatological texts excerpted in the lectionary. Their resonances with what has been accomplished in Christ should be explained, but what is now unfinished and still anticipated in the eschatological future must also be made clear.

4. Interpretations of the Bible That Produce Negative Attitudes Toward Jews or Judaism Are in Error.

The ways in which Christians actualize biblical texts that refer to Jews and Judaism is of particular importance. As they enter into dialogue with the world of the scriptural writers, modern preachers, teachers, and readers must be careful not to confuse words originally written during heated exchanges with timeless truths of the faith. The Executive Committee of the World Council of Churches has expressed it concisely: "The Church must learn so to preach and teach the Gospel as to make sure that it cannot be used towards contempt for Judaism and against the Jewish people."[56]

The Pontifical Biblical Commission expressed the same idea in its 1992 instruction:

Clearly to be rejected also is every attempt at actualization set in a direction contrary to evangelical justice and charity, such as, for example, the use of the Bible to justify racial segregation, anti-Semitism or sexism whether on the part of men or of women.

Particular attention is necessary according to the spirit of the Second Vatican Council (*Nostra Aetate*, 4), to avoid absolutely any actualization of certain texts of the New [Christian] Testament which could provoke or reinforce unfavorable attitudes to the Jewish people. The tragic events of the past must, on the contrary, impel all to keep unceasingly in mind that, according to the New [Christian] Testament, the Jews remain "beloved" of God, "since the gifts and calling of God are irrevocable." (Rom 11:28–29)[57]

Such logic must inevitably apply to how Christians interpret the Shared Testament as well. The way in which the Shared Testament is related to the Christian Testament must not inadvertently promote demeaning attitudes about the Jewish tradition or people. With respect to preaching or teaching from the lectionary, then, approaches that empty the Shared Testament of its inspired character or reduce it to a foreshadowing of Christianity violate this principle, which disallows actualizations unfavorable to Judaism.

D. Conclusion

In order to illustrate how to teach and preach the first reading texts as a Shared Testament, the main part of this volume will consider five sets of lectionary reading from four liturgical seasons in the church year: Advent, Christmas, Lent, and Easter. To sum up the previous section, these passages will be explored according to the following principles of critical scriptural interpretation. First, the meaning of the Shared Testament reading in its own historical and social context will be summarized. Second, the Christian Testament's rereading of that passage in reference to Christ will be brought out in ways that preserve the integrity of both Testaments. Third, possible modern actualizations of the lectionary readings will be suggested. Those with eschatological aspects will be addressed both from realized and unfinished perspectives. Complete lessons or sermons will not be devised, but ideas for their development will be offered. In all cases an accurate and affirming approach to the Jewish people and tradition will be followed, because, to paraphrase Pope John Paul II, Jews are the dearly beloved brothers and sisters of Christians, our elder siblings who introduced the church to covenantal life with God.[58]

NOTES

1. Pope John Paul II, "Address to the Pontifical Biblical Commission," *L'Osservatore Romano* (April 23, 1997), 2.

2. Ibid.

3. See in particular the research of Robert L. Wilken, *The Christians as the Romans Saw Them* (New Haven, Conn.: Yale University Press, 1984); *John Chrysostom and the Jews: Rhetoric and Reality in the Late Fourth Century* (Berkeley and Los Angeles: University of California Press, 1983); and *Judaism and the Early Christian Mind: A Study of Cyril of Alexandria's Exegesis and Theology* (New Haven, Conn.: Yale University Press, 1971).

4. Augustine of Hippo, *De Catechizandis Rudibus*, 3/5, trans. Joseph Patrick Christopher (Washington, D.C.: The Catholic University of America, 1926).

5. Ibid., 4/8.

6. Robert M. Grant with David Tracy, *A Short History of Biblical Interpretation*, 2d ed. (Philadelphia: Fortress Press, 1984), 85.

7. B.C.E. means Before the Common Era. Together with C.E. (the Common Era), it offers alternative terminology to the traditional Christian B.C. (before Christ) and A.D. (Anno Domini, in the year of the Lord). Such non-christological conventions are appropriate in the context of reconsidering the non-christological meanings of the scriptures from ancient Israel.

8. Nostra Aetate, 4, in Vatican Council II, *The Basic Sixteen Documents: Constitutions, Decrees, Declarations*, ed. Austin Flannery (New York: Costello Publishing, 1996).

9. 199th General Assembly of the Presbyterian Church USA, "A Theological Understanding of the Relationship Between Christians and Jews" (1987), Affirmation 5.

10. Several official documents from various Christian bodies will be cited below. There is a greater number of Roman Catholic texts mentioned. This is the result of Catholic polity. Its

centralized teaching office naturally lends itself to the produc-
tion of authoritative instructions. This is not the case in more
congregationally based polities that understand ecclesial authority differently. Not surprisingly, the more numerous Catholic
texts have also offered more comments on the scriptural topics
that are relevant to this consideration of the lectionary.

11. Vatican Commission for Religious Relations with
the Jews, "Notes on the Correct Way to Present the Jews and
Judaism in Preaching and Catechesis in the Roman Catholic
Church," II, 6–7; *Origins* 15/7 (July 4, 1985).

12. Bishops' Committee on the Liturgy, National Con-
ference of Catholic Bishops, *God's Mercy Endures Forever:
Guidelines on the Presentation of Jews and Judaism in Catholic
Preaching* (Washington, D.C.: U.S.C.C., 1988), 31, a, c.

13. Ibid., 15.

14. Pope John Paul II, "Address to the Pontifical Biblical Commission," 2.

15. This section is a revision of an unpublished essay
called "Testamental Terminology" that was prepared for the
August 9–12, 1997 meeting of the Continuing Seminar on
Biblical Issues in Jewish-Christian Relations of the Catholic
Biblical Association of America. I am indebted to the members
of that seminar for helping to refine certain points made in the
original paper.

16. Two books devoted to aspects of these issues are
Roger Brooks and John J. Collins, eds., *Hebrew Bible or Old Tes-
tament?: Studying the Bible in Judaism and Christianity* (Notre
Dame, Ind.: University of Notre Dame Press, 1990), and Jon D.
Levenson, *The Hebrew Bible, the Old Testament, and Historical
Criticism* (Louisville, Ky.: Westminster/John Knox Press, 1993).

17. John Paul II, "To the Jewish Community of Aus-
tralia" (November 26, 1986), in *Spiritual Pilgrimage: Pope John
Paul II—Texts on Jews and Judaism 1979–1995*, ed. Eugene J.
Fisher and Leon Klenicki (New York: Crossroad, 1995), 83.

18. Vatican Commission for Religious Relations with the Jews, "Notes on the Correct Way to Present the Jews and Judaism in Preaching and Catechesis in the Roman Catholic Church," n. 1. Italics in original.

19. Synod of the Evangelical Church of the Rhineland, "Towards Renovation of the Relationship of Christians and Jews" (1980), 7, in World Council of Churches, *The Theology of the Churches and the Jewish People* (Geneva: WCC Publications, 1988), 93.

20. Pontifical Biblical Commission, "The Bible and Christology," 1.2.1, in Joseph A. Fitzmyer, *Scripture and Christology: A Statement of the Biblical Commission with a Commentary* (Mahwah, N.J.: Paulist Press, 1986).

21. Pontifical Biblical Commission, "The Interpretation of the Bible in the Church," *Origins* 23/29 (January 26, 1994): III, 2, 3.

22. André Lacocque, "The 'Old Testament' in the Protestant Tradition," in *Biblical Studies: Meeting Ground of Jews and Christians*, ed. Lawrence Boadt, Helga Croner, and Leon Klenicki (Ramsey, N.J.: Paulist Press/Stimulus Books, 1980), 121.

23. Elisabeth Schüssler Fiorenza, *Jesus—Miriam's Child, Sophia's Prophet: Critical Issues in Feminist Christology* (New York: Continuum, 1984), 193, n. 8.

24. James A. Sanders, "First Testament and Second," *Biblical Theology Bulletin* 17/2 (April 1987): 47–49.

25. This term is the most widely used alternative. One example is Paul Van Buren, *A Theology of the Jewish-Christian Reality*, vol. 1, *Discerning the Way* (New York: Seabury, 1980), 23.

26. Ibid.

27. Schüssler Fiorenza, *Jesus*, 193, n. 8.

28. Sanders, "First Testament and Second."

29. For a convenient survey of the debate, see the exchange between Christopher R. Seitz, "Old Testament or

Hebrew Bible?: Some Theological Considerations," *Pro Ecclesia* 5/3 (Summer 1996): 292–303, and Eugene J. Fisher, "Correspondence: A Reply to Christopher Seitz," *Pro Ecclesia* 6/2: 133–36. Another dialogue occurred between Lawrence Boadt, "Old Testament or Hebrew Scriptures?," *New Theology Review* 4/4 (November 1991): 92–96, and Eugene J. Fisher, "Old Testament—An Outdated Term: A Response to Fr. Boadt," *New Theology Review* 5/3 (August 1992): 104–6.

30. William Safire, "On Language: The New Old Testament," *The New York Times Magazine* (May 25, 1997), 20.

31. Sixteenth General Synod of the United Church of Christ, USA, "The Relationship Between the United Church of Christ and the Jewish Community" (1987), available on various Internet websites. See also, by way of a few additional examples out of many, The Texas Conference of Churches, "Dialogue: A Contemporary Alternative to Proselytization" (1982), in World Council of Churches, *The Theology of the Churches and the Jewish People*, 96; General Assembly of the Presbyterian Church (USA), "A Theological Understanding of the Relationship Between Christians and Jews" (1987), in ibid., 110–12; General Convention of the Episcopal Church (USA), "Guidelines for Christian-Jewish Relations" (1988), II, 5–8.

32. Vatican Commission for Religious Relations with the Jews, "Guidelines and Suggestions for Implementing the Conciliar Declaration *Nostra Aetate* (no. 4)" (1974), Preamble, in *In Our Time: The Flowering of Jewish and Catholic Dialogue*, ed. Eugene J. Fisher and Leon Klenicki (Mahwah, N.J.: Paulist Press/Stimulus Books, 1990), 32.

33. Vatican Commission for Religious Relations with the Jews, "Notes on the Correct Way to Present the Jews and Judaism in Preaching and Catechesis in the Roman Catholic Church," VI, 25.

34. John Paul II, "To Christian Experts in Jewish-Christian Relations" (March 6, 1982), in Fisher and Klenicki, *Spiritual Pilgrimage*, 19.

35. The Executive Committee of the World Council of Churches, "Ecumenical Considerations on Jewish-Christian Dialogue" (1982), 2.12, in World Council of Churches, *The Theology of the Churches and the Jewish People*, 39.

36. Bishops' Committee on the Liturgy, *God's Mercy Endures Forever*, 31, I. Note the testamental terminology employed.

37. Vatican Commission for Religious Relations with the Jews, "Guidelines and Suggestions for Implementing the Conciliar Declaration *Nostra Aetate* (no. 4)," II, in Fisher and Klenicki, *In Our Time*, 33.

38. Vatican Commission for Religious Relations with the Jews, "Notes on the Correct Way to Present the Jews and Judaism in Preaching and Catechesis in the Roman Catholic Church," II, 6–7.

39. Ibid.

40. Texas Conference of Churches, "Dialogue: A Contemporary Alternative to Proselytization" (1982), II, C, D.

41. Vatican Commission for Religious Relations with the Jews, "Notes on the Correct Way to Present the Jews and Judaism in Preaching and Catechesis in the Roman Catholic Church," I, 2.

42. John Paul II, "To the Jewish Community in Rome" (April 13, 1986), in Fisher and Klenicki, *Spiritual Pilgrimage*, 63.

43. My thanks to David P. Efroymson for making this objection.

44. Indeed, there is another theological problem lurking even with non-supersessionist understandings of *Old Covenant* and *New Covenant*. The terms might suggest that the church and Judaism are "two parallel ways of salvation," an approach

criticized by the Vatican (see Vatican Commission for Religious Relations with the Jews, "Notes on the Correct Way to Present the Jews and Judaism in Preaching and Catechesis in the Roman Catholic Church," I, 7).

45. Second Vatican Council, *Dei Verbum*, 12, in Flannery, Vatican Council II, *The Basic Sixteen Documents*.

46. Pontifical Biblical Commission, "The Interpretation of the Bible in the Church," III, in *Origins* 23/29 (January 6, 1994), 497–525.

47. Sandra M. Schneiders, *The Revelatory Text: Interpreting the New Testament as Sacred Scripture*, 2d ed. (Collegeville, Minn.: The Liturgical Press, 1999), 146.

48. Ibid., 148.

49. Vatican Commission for Religious Relations with the Jews, "Guidelines and Suggestions for Implementing the Conciliar Declaration *Nostra Aetate* (no. 4)," II, in Fisher and Klenicki, *In Our Time*, 33.

50. Vatican Commission for Religious Relations with the Jews, "Notes on the Correct Way to Present the Jews and Judaism in Preaching and Catechesis in the Roman Catholic Church," II, 6–7.

51. Pontifical Biblical Commission, "The Interpretation of the Bible in the Church," III, A, 1.

52. Ibid.

53. For details about the evangelists use of Psalm 22, see Raymond E. Brown, *The Death of the Messiah* (New York: Doubleday, 1994), 1455–65.

54. Pontifical Biblical Commission, "The Interpretation of the Bible in the Church," III, A, 3.

55. Bishops' Committee on the Liturgy, *God's Mercy Endures Forever*, 11.

56. WCC Executive Committee, "Ecumenical Considerations," 3.2, in World Council of Churches, *The Theology of the Churches and the Jewish People*, 41.

57. Pontifical Biblical Commission, "The Interpretation of the Bible in the Church," IV, A, 3.

58. John Paul II, "To the Jewish Community in Rome" (April 13, 1986), in Fisher and Klenicki, *Spiritual Pilgrimage*, p. 63.

SAMPLE TEXTS
AND COMMENTARIES

A. Advent—Fourth Sunday of Advent (Cycle A)

Reading 1: Isaiah 7:10–14

10 Again the LORD spoke to Ahaz, saying, ¹¹Ask a sign of the LORD your God; let it be deep as Sheol or high as heaven. ¹²But Ahaz said, I will not ask, and I will not put the LORD to the test. ¹³Then Isaiah said: "Hear then, O house of David! Is it too little for you to weary mortals, that you weary my God also? ¹⁴Therefore the Lord himself will give you a sign. Look, the young woman [some translations: "virgin"] is with child and shall bear a son, and shall name him Immanuel.

Reading 2: Romans 1:1–7

1 Paul, a servant of Jesus Christ, called to be an apostle, set apart for the gospel of God, ²which he promised beforehand through his prophets in the holy scriptures, ³the gospel concerning his Son, who was descended from David according to the flesh ⁴and was declared to be Son of God with power according to the spirit of holiness by resurrection from the dead, Jesus Christ our Lord, ⁵through whom we have received grace and apostleship to bring about the obedience of faith among all the Gentiles for the sake of his name, ⁶including yourselves who are called to belong to Jesus Christ,

7 To all God's beloved in Rome, who are called to be saints:

Grace to you and peace from God our Father and the Lord Jesus Christ.

Gospel: Matthew 1:18–24

18 Now the birth of Jesus the Messiah took place in this way. When his mother Mary had been engaged to Joseph, but

before they lived together, she was found to be with child from the Holy Spirit. [19]Her husband Joseph, being a righteous man and unwilling to expose her to public disgrace, planned to dismiss her quietly. [20]But just when he had resolved to do this, an angel of the Lord appeared to him in a dream and said, "Joseph, son of David, do not be afraid to take Mary as your wife, for the child conceived in her is from the Holy Spirit. [21]She will bear a son, and you are to name him Jesus, for he will save his people from their sins." [22]All this took place to fulfill what had been spoken by the Lord through the prophet:

[23] "Look, the virgin shall conceive and bear a son,
    and they shall name him Emmanuel,"

which means, "God is with us." [24]When Joseph awoke from sleep, he did as the angel of the Lord commanded him; he took her as his wife.

Commentary

The Shared Testament reading comes from the prophet Isaiah of Jerusalem, also known as First Isaiah. He prophesied toward the end of the eighth century B.C.E., an unsettled time marked by the growing power of the empire of Assyria. This lectionary selection refers to a rather specific geo-political event that occurred during Isaiah's career. Unfortunately, the lectionary excerpts the Isaian text without the historical benchmarks needed to understand the prophet's point in its original setting.

Around 735 B.C.E. some local kingdoms decided to unite to resist the power of the Assyrian Empire. Included in this alliance was the northern Hebrew kingdom of Israel (also called Ephraim) with its capital in Samaria and the kingdom of Syria (also called Aram) with its capital in Damascus. The kings of these countries pressured King Ahaz in Jerusalem to bring Judea into their coalition. Ahaz was not inclined to join the revolt. Instead, he intended to ingratiate himself to Assyria by warning the emperor of the plot and by asking for his help against the attacks that Israel and Syria began making on Judea. This conflict is known as the Syro-Ephraimite War.

The prophet Isaiah, who seems to have functioned as a royal counselor, opposed such overtures to Assyria. He urged King Ahaz to rely only on the Lord. This is the context for the sign with which Isaiah confronts Ahaz. Just as he had given other children symbolic names (see Isaiah 7:3 and 8:1–4), so now Isaiah names an unborn child "God is with us." His intentions are best seen by considering the three verses following the lectionary excerpt:

> **7** [14]Therefore the Lord himself will give you a sign. Look, the young woman is with child and shall bear a son, and shall name him Immanuel. [15]He shall eat curds and honey by the time he knows how to refuse the evil and choose the good. [16]For before the child knows how to refuse the evil and choose the good, the land before whose two kings you are in dread will be deserted. [17]The LORD will bring on you and on your people and on your ancestral house such days as have not come since the day that Ephraim departed from Judah—the king of Assyria.

The prophet's message is that Ahaz should sit tight. He should neither join the revolt nor submit to Assyria. He should trust that God is present. The sign is this—by the time a pregnant woman's child is able to know right from wrong, Syria and Israel will be destroyed by the far greater threat of Assyria. The reality that God is with us [the Judeans] will then be abundantly clear. This ongoing divine presence demands the king's complete loyalty to God during the time of Assyria's dominance. According to 2 Kings 16:7–9, however, Ahaz did not heed Isaiah's advice.

There is an important complication of translation in this passage. The Hebrew word *almah* does not confirm or deny virginity but simply means "young woman." In the context of the Syro-Ephraimite War, the woman is likely one of Ahaz's wives, and the child may well be his son, the future King Hezekiah, remembered in the Bible as one of Judah's better kings and the likely basis of the ideal monarch of Isaiah 9:1–7. When Isaiah was translated as part of the Greek Septuagint, *almah* became *parthenos*, a word that does denote virginity. The miraculous element of this rendering combined with the expectation of an ideal king in Isaiah 9:1–7 set the stage for the later rereading of Isaiah by the evangelist Matthew.

For Isaiah of Jerusalem, however, the emphasis was on the saving presence of God. Kings of Judah should not be blown this way and that by the current international crisis but should be loyal to the God-who-is-with-us and who will see Judah through intrigues and empires.

Writing about eight hundred years later, the evangelist Matthew begins his presentation of the meaning of the life of Jesus with a recounting of his birth. For Matthew, Jesus reprises the story of Israel in his person. The story of Jesus' birth is full of allusions to famous ancestors such as Joseph the dreamer and Moses the lawgiver. Jesus' birth is introduced by a genealogy that notably includes four famous women with unusual sexual histories, just as his own mother Mary is nearly divorced by her fiancé, Joseph. This is Matthew's way of saying that God's long story with Israel is coming to a focal point in the birth of this child. Matthew makes this assertion explicitly with a series of "fulfillment passages" that draw upon Israel's scriptures in order to impart the significance of Jesus.

Matthew's use of Isaiah's Emmanuel name might at first seem odd. The text says that "they shall name him Emmanuel," but no character in the infancy narrative refers to Jesus as God-is-with-us. In fact, the child is named Jesus.

Matthew draws upon Isaiah to explain the identity of the child but also to prepare for the conclusion of his gospel narrative. The last sentence in the Gospel of Matthew is the statement by the raised and glorified Jesus, "And remember, *I am with you* always, to the end of the age" (28:20). That is why, for Matthew, Isaiah 7:14 is so meaningful. Matthew and his church community both sense the presence of God in their communion with the Lord Jesus. They find the name Emmanuel particularly meaningful to their experience of Christ. God is with them through the Crucified and Raised One. This perception informs Matthew's portrayal of the entire story of Jesus, including the circumstances of his birth. The Septuagint translation that Matthew uses makes the link to Jesus even more apt. For Matthew, God-is-with-us more profoundly than ever before. Through the virginal conception of Jesus, the God who has always been present to Israel, as Isaiah testified, now becomes directly present to the people. For Matthew, Isaiah's words were never more true. They have been fulfilled, reached their ultimate application, in Jesus.

It is important not to present Isaiah as simply predicting the birth of Jesus. The prophet was addressing the needs of his own time and perceived a timeless truth about God's relationship with those bonded in divine covenant—God will always be there. Matthew, to be sure, sees this truth most intensely manifested in Jesus Christ, but Isaiah's insight is not restricted either to his own situation with Ahaz or its Matthean application to Jesus' birth. God is still with God's people and will always be with them. Biblical prophecy is not a time-limited prediction but an inspired insight that transcends all historical moments.

Actualization

These considerations offer cues as to how we might actualize these two passages today. Clearly, both are concerned with the faithful presence of God. Isaiah was certain that God was present during Judah's political trials. He believed that God would always be present to Israel. Matthew was convinced that God was present in the birth of Jesus and that God would always be present to the church through its Risen Lord. To add in the second lectionary reading, Paul discerned that God had an ongoing plan for humanity that was being advanced in his own day. All three inspired writers perceived God acting in their lives and histories.

Are we similarly attuned to detecting God at work? Are we able to discover Isaiah's insight being fulfilled again and again in our own times? Are we as confident that God is present with us? This is one challenge that the Advent season poses to Christians—to reaffirm our conviction that God is with us and will continue to be with us in the unfolding of our own lives and in the ongoing history of all humanity.

B. Christmas—Second Sunday after Christmas (Cycles A, B, C)

Reading 1: Sirach 24:1–4, 8–12

Wisdom praises herself,
  and tells of her glory in the midst of her people.
² In the assembly of the Most High she opens her mouth,
  and in the presence of his hosts she tells of her glory:
³ "I came forth from the mouth of the Most High,
  and covered the earth like a mist.
⁴ I dwelt in the highest heavens,
  and my throne was in a pillar of cloud.
⁸ "Then the Creator of all things gave me a command,
  and my Creator chose the place for my tent.
 He said, 'Make your dwelling in Jacob,
  and in Israel receive your inheritance.'
⁹ Before the ages, in the beginning, he created me,
  and for all the ages I shall not cease to be.
¹⁰ In the holy tent I ministered before him,
  and so I was established in Zion.
¹¹ Thus in the beloved city he gave me a resting place,
  and in Jerusalem was my domain.
¹² I took root in an honored people,
  in the portion of the Lord, his heritage."

Reading 2: Ephesians 1:3–6, 15–18

3 Blessed be the God and Father of our Lord Jesus Christ, who has blessed us in Christ with every spiritual blessing in the heavenly places, ⁴just as he chose us in Christ before the foundation of the world to be holy and blameless before him in love. ⁵He destined us for adoption as his children through Jesus Christ, according to the good pleasure of his

will, ⁶to the praise of his glorious grace that he freely bestowed on us in the Beloved.

15 I have heard of your faith in the Lord Jesus and your love toward all the saints, and for this reason ¹⁶I do not cease to give thanks for you as I remember you in my prayers. ¹⁷I pray that the God of our Lord Jesus Christ, the Father of glory, may give you a spirit of wisdom and revelation as you come to know him, ¹⁸so that, with the eyes of your heart enlightened, you may know what is the hope to which he has called you, what are the riches of his glorious inheritance among the saints.

Gospel: John 1:1–18

1 In the beginning was the Word, and the Word was with God, and the Word was God. ²He was in the beginning with God. ³All things came into being through him, and without him not one thing came into being. What has come into being ⁴in him was life, and the life was the light of all people. ⁵The light shines in the darkness, and the darkness did not overcome it.

6 There was a man sent from God, whose name was John. ⁷He came as a witness to testify to the light, so that all might believe through him. ⁸He himself was not the light, but he came to testify to the light. ⁹The true light, which enlightens everyone, was coming into the world.

10 He was in the world, and the world came into being through him; yet the world did not know him. ¹¹He came to what was his own, and his own people did not accept him. ¹²But to all who received him, who believed in his name, he gave power to become children of God, ¹³who were born, not of blood or of the will of the flesh or of the will of man, but of God.

14 And the Word became flesh and lived among us, and we have seen his glory, the glory as of a father's only son, full of

grace and truth. [15](John testified to him and cried out, "This was he of whom I said, 'He who comes after me ranks ahead of me because he was before me.'") [16]From his fullness we have all received, grace upon grace. [17]The law indeed was given through Moses; grace and truth came through Jesus Christ. [18]No one has ever seen God. It is God the only Son, who is close to the Father's heart, who has made him known.

Commentary

The Shared Testament passage is from a deutero-canonical book that is not considered scriptural by Jews and most Protestant denominations. Composed around 185 B.C.E. by a teacher in Jerusalem, the book seeks to illustrate that the wisdom of the Jewish tradition is superior to that of the widespread and influential Greek culture. In a striking poem that is excerpted in this reading, Ben Sirach praises the Wisdom of God, a feminine personification of God's divine plan for all of creation.

Wisdom describes herself as created by God's mouth and as pervading all the world from the depths of the sea to the heights of the heavens (Sir 24:4–6, not included in the lection). She uses language that recalls important texts from the Torah. She covers "the earth like a mist," an allusion to God's spirit hovering over the primeval universe (Gn 1:2). Her throne as "a pillar of cloud" is reminiscent of the "pillar of cloud" that guided Israel during the Exodus (Ex 13:21–22). These images, together with her address before the heavenly court in the assembly of the Most High, indicate that her dwelling place is with God and that she has been instrumental in implementing divine designs throughout time.

After searching for an abode among humanity (Sir 24:7), God decrees that she should dwell among the people Israel. She "pitches her tent" in Jerusalem and serves God in the Temple, probably by regulating proper worship (24:10). Thus, true wisdom, the Wisdom of God, is seen by Ben Sirah as having been given by God to Israel. She dwells both with God and within the Temple, and is articulated verbally in the Torah, "the book of the covenant of the Most High God" (24:23). God abides with Israel and within Israel's worship and sacred texts. The wisdom that Israel possesses, then, is superior to that of the pagan world because it came as a gift from God.

This poetic language is taken up in the hymn that comprises the prologue of the Gospel of John. The image of God's Wisdom is applied to Jesus through the masculine Greek term for "word," *logos*. This metaphor contributes the correct gender in respect to Jesus, but, more important, it makes connections with Greek philosophical ideas about the *logos* who imparts divine order to the cosmos. *Logos*, then, provides links with the Hellenistic world into which the church is moving, but John's prologue is primarily rooted in the Jewish tradition's ideas about the creative Word of God and the revealing Wisdom of God.

And so, the Word abides with God before time itself has begun. Just as divine Wisdom came from the mouth of God and pervaded creation, so for the prologue, creation comes into being through the agency of the divine Word. Just as Wisdom searched the world for a dwelling among humanity, so the Word is unknown by the world. Whereas, Wisdom "pitched her tent" in Temple and Torah, the Word became flesh, became human, and, following the Greek literally, "tabernacled" or "pitched his tent among us" (Jn 1:14). This incarnate Wisdom/Word of God reveals God fully. The hymn concludes by contrasting the Law of Moses, which was indeed of divine origin, with the more direct disclosure provided by Jesus Christ, the Word who dwelt with God and revealed God in the flesh (1:17–18).

In terms of Jewish and Christian relations today, care is needed with those verses of the prologue that reflect the polemical social setting of this evangelist and that, in the words of the Pontifical Biblical Commission, "could provoke or reinforce unfavorable attitudes to the Jewish people."[1] This involves to some extent the Moses-Jesus comparison in 1:17–18 but more directly concerns "He came to what was his own, and his own people did not accept him" (1:11).

Here the evangelist is tapping the Jewish tradition that God's Wisdom frequently meets with rejection even within Israel. For example, one deutero-canonical work observes that Israel was exiled because "you have forsaken the fountain of wisdom" (Bar 3:12) and an apocryphal text moans that "Wisdom came to make her dwelling place among the children of men and found no dwelling place" (Enoch 42:2).[2] Given this tradition, it is not surprising that the incarnated Wisdom/Word of God would be portrayed as encountering rejection by both the world and Israel.

However, this theme is heightened by the social setting of this evangelist. His is a church whose Jewish members have recently faced expulsion from the local synagogue (Jn 9:22; 12:42; 16:2). This conflict seems centered on the Johannine community's proclamation of Jesus in an exalted language that strikes the synagogue as a denial of monotheism (e.g., 5:18). The pain of their ejection produces an angry tone in the gospel, repeatedly evidenced, for example, in its sarcastic references to "the Jews" (sometimes probably "Judeans") as opponents of Jesus, even though Jesus himself and all his followers were themselves Jews.

This polemic somewhat informs the prologue's rejection-of-Wisdom motif and the Moses-Jesus comparison. The Incarnate Word/Wisdom from God has not been accepted by his own people even though he reveals God more directly than Moses. Although relatively mild in contrast to other gospel passages (e.g., 8:44), preachers and teachers should reckon with the polemic nonetheless.

Actualization

These lectionary selections might be actualized in this way. All three of the day's lections express the belief that God is at work in everything that exists. The Shared Testament reading from Sirach poetically describes the Wisdom of God as imbuing everything that the Creator builds and sustains. The intentions and desires of God are especially revealed to the people of Israel. Through their worship of God in the Temple and through their observance of God's teachings in the Torah, the Jewish people brought into the world a deep relationship with the one Creator of all. To this day they have a Wisdom that gives meaning to life and holiness to human pursuits.

For the writer of the Gospel of John, this Wisdom has become personified in a fleshly way in the life and death of Jesus Christ. Those who come to know Jesus enter into a deep relationship with the divine and become God's adopted children. The divine wish that all humanity become God's children is also noted by the author of the letter to the Ephesians. As both that letter and John's gospel make clear, friendship with Jesus requires a life based on love in service to one another. This lifestyle will help to bring about God's plans for the world.

However, such a holy lifestyle, if intensely pursued, often meets with rejection by the world and occasionally even with disdain from people of faith. As both the Shared Testament and the Christian Testament are aware, God's Wisdom does not always find a home even among religious communities—even among us. In the words of Ephesians, do we fully understand the glorious hope to which we have been called? Do we accept the gift of the spirit of Wisdom that we have been given? Do we really believe in the "glorious inheritance" to which we have been called, even on those days when the whole world seems to be turning against us?

On Christmas Day, it is fitting to wonder about the birth of the physical embodiment of God's plans for humanity and for the world. Let us marvel at how immersed with human lives God has always been—from creation, to the establishing of the unending covenant with the people of Israel, to the birth of the revealing Word, Jesus Christ, and to God's saving deeds in the world today. The church has experienced and continues to know Jesus as the ultimate expression of God's continual re-creation of the world. The Gospel of John would have each of us personally come to know Jesus in this way so that his life can shape our own.

C. Lent—Second Sunday of Lent (Cycle B)

Reading 1: Genesis 22:1–2, 9, 10–13, 15–18

22 After these things God tested Abraham. He said to him, "Abraham!" And he said, "Here I am." [2] He said, "Take your son, your only son Isaac, whom you love, and go to the land of Moriah, and offer him there as a burnt offering on one of the mountains that I shall show you."

9 When they came to the place that God had shown him, Abraham built an altar there and laid the wood in order. [10]Then Abraham reached out his hand and took the knife to kill his son. [11]But the angel of the LORD called to him from heaven, and said, "Abraham, Abraham!" And he said, "Here I am." [12]He said, "Do not lay your hand on the boy or do anything to him; for now I know that you fear God, since you have not withheld your son, your only son, from me." [13]And Abraham looked up and saw a ram, caught in a thicket by its horns. Abraham went and took the ram and offered it up as a burnt offering instead of his son.

15 The angel of the LORD called to Abraham a second time from heaven, [16]and said, "By myself I have sworn, says the LORD: Because you have done this, and have not withheld your son, your only son, [17]I will indeed bless you, and I will make your offspring as numerous as the stars of heaven and as the sand that is on the seashore. And your offspring shall possess the gate of their enemies, [18]and by your offspring shall all the nations of the earth gain blessing for themselves, because you have obeyed my voice."

Reading 2: Romans 8:31–34

31 What then are we to say about these things? If God is for us, who is against us? [32]He who did not withhold his own

Son, but gave him up for all of us, will he not with him also give us everything else? ³³Who will bring any charge against God's elect? It is God who justifies. ³⁴Who is to condemn? It is Christ Jesus, who died, yes, who was raised, who is at the right hand of God, who indeed intercedes for us.

Gospel: Mark 9:2–10

2 Jesus took with him Peter and James and John, and led them up a high mountain apart, by themselves. And he was transfigured before them, ³and his clothes became dazzling white, such as no one on earth could bleach them. ⁴And there appeared to them Elijah with Moses, who were talking with Jesus. ⁵Then Peter said to Jesus, "Rabbi, it is good for us to be here; let us make three dwellings, one for you, one for Moses, and one for Elijah." ⁶He did not know what to say, for they were terrified. ⁷Then a cloud overshadowed them, and from the cloud there came a voice, "This is my Son, the Beloved; listen to him!" ⁸Suddenly when they looked around, they saw no one with them any more, but only Jesus.

9 As they were coming down the mountain, he ordered them to tell no one about what they had seen, until after the Son of Man had risen from the dead. ¹⁰So they kept the matter to themselves, questioning what this rising from the dead could mean.

Commentary

The story of the near-sacrifice of Isaac is one of the most powerful scenes in the Shared Testament. It has been a source of continuous reflection and commentary in the Jewish and Christian traditions, and among Islamic interpreters as well.

Source critics typically see two layers of development in the passage. Genesis 22:1–13 is often associated with the Elohist source, written in the north kingdom of Israel around 900 B.C.E., while verses 14–19 are thought to be a later addition, possibly during the reign of King Hezekiah around 700 B.C.E.[3]

Although often understood as the Hebrew rejection of child sacrifice, the original text may not have shared the later Hebrew tradition's repudiation of that practice. Nothing in the passage suggests that God's initial demand is improper or unthinkable. In fact, Abraham is ultimately praised for his willingness to comply with the command—an odd commendation if the passage intended to forbid child sacrifice.[4]

The original text may primarily have aimed to highlight Abraham's total dedication to God. "Abraham's obedience is absolute and uncompromising. Just as the trial begins with 'God['s] put[ting] Abraham to the test' with no mention of Isaac, so does it end with God's acknowledgment that Abraham fears him without any mention of Isaac's name or the countervailing force of his paternal affection for the beloved son whom he had refused to withhold (v. 12)."[5] The story is part of a literary pattern in the Elohist tradition—a concern for jeopardy to children—and a conviction that fear of the Lord is the only proper course of action.[6]

The passage also recalls the Exodus event. Both on Mount Moriah and in Egypt the firstborn are preserved from death through the blood of sacrificial lambs and so are able to perpetuate the promises given to ancestors.

In the later Jewish tradition the episode is known as the *Aqedah*—the "binding" of Isaac. Over the centuries rabbis commented on this passage in remarkable ways. Some imagined that Abraham actually slew Isaac, whom God then resurrected. Others speculated that Isaac was consumed by the sacrificial fires that sprang up and immolated him before Abraham could remove him from the wood after God's messenger had commanded him to stay his hand. God, however, restored his ashes to life again. Still other rabbis held that

Abraham was so driven by God's command that he sought to slay his son a second time after his resurrection. This led to God's angelic messenger intervening for a second time. Some of these midrashim, or imaginative expansions of the biblical text, may have been sparked by the "Sanctification of the Name," the faithful deaths of Jewish martyrs who died in steadfast witness to the sovereignty of the One. Those Jews who preferred death at the hands of Romans (or later Christians) rather than betray their covenant with the God of Israel were associated with the example of Abraham, who also sacrificed his son so that God's name might be glorified. The elaboration of the biblical tale to include Isaac's resurrection also offered hope to the martyrs and their families that the God of life would not abandon them.[7]

In Christianity a typological reading of the sacrifice of Isaac prevailed. Isaac and Jesus were paired as the beloved sons who carried the wood to their own sacrifices according to the will of their fathers. Isaac was understood as a "type" whose interrupted sacrifice foreshadowed the perfect sacrifice of Christ on the cross.

There is a further element to this passage that provides a linkage to the lectionary's gospel selection. Ironically, the linking verses, 8 and 14, are not included in the Shared Testament lection. These verses, usually taken to be later additions to the original episode, offer word plays on the Hebrew word meaning "to see." Taking a cue from verse 8, in which Abraham tells his son, literally, that "God will see to the sheep," verse 14 explains that "Abraham called that place 'The Lord will see' *[Yhwh-yireh]*," as it is said to this day, "On the mount of the Lord, God sees" or "there is vision." The name Moriah itself may be a part of the word play, possibly meaning "God sees." "The mount of the Lord" is in all likelihood an allusion to the Temple Mount in Jerusalem where lamb sacrifices occurred for centuries. In the Temple precincts, in which the divine

Presence or Name dwelt, God could be encountered or "seen" through the Temple rituals, and God, in turn, "saw" the worship offered there.

The gospel reading presents another vision on what could be called a "mount of the Lord." After presenting the first of three predictions of his suffering and death (Mk 8:31; 9:30–31; 10:32–35), the Gospel of Mark describes three of Jesus' disciples, upon a high mountain, experiencing a vision of him in transcendent glory. They have an opportunity of seeing past the imminent threat of Jesus' death to a glimpse of the divine identity of Jesus as God's beloved Son. This scene relates to one of Mark's principal themes—Jesus' divine Sonship is manifest only in his death on the cross in which Jesus will "give his life as a ransom for many" (Mk 10:45).

Actualization

In preaching or teaching about these paired lections, care should be taken to portray the readings as signs of a recurrent pattern of divine activity. Thus, following the cue of the second reading, which stresses God's boundless love, one could expand upon how God will not let the death of either Isaac or Jesus bring their stories to an end. They both are destined in God's design to be the foundations of faith communities. Isaac will further the divine promises to Abraham to form the people of Israel, while the resurrection of Jesus will summon the church into existence.

One could also focus on the faithfulness of Abraham and Jesus as models of how people living in covenant with God should live. Both Abraham and Jesus remained steadfast in following God's will, even when the prospect of death seemed to make such a commitment look self-defeating and disastrous. Abraham risked everything in following God's will, even the death of all his hopes for numerous descendants. Jesus put his entire life, confronting death itself, in the service of the coming of God's kingdom. Their fidelity was instrumental in bringing great blessing into the world. Such examples challenge the faithful today to consider their own commitments to God. To what extent are we prepared to commit our hopes and our lives to furthering God's plans for the world?

D. Lent—Fifth Sunday of Lent (Cycle B)

Reading 1: Jeremiah 31:31–34

31 The days are surely coming, says the LORD, when I will make a new covenant with the house of Israel and the house of Judah. ³²It will not be like the covenant that I made with their ancestors when I took them by the hand to bring them out of the land of Egypt—a covenant that they broke, though I was their husband, says the LORD. ³³But this is the covenant that I will make with the house of Israel after those days, says the LORD: I will put my law within them, and I will write it on their hearts; and I will be their God, and they shall be my people. ³⁴No longer shall they teach one another, or say to each other, "Know the LORD," for they shall all know me, from the least of them to the greatest, says the LORD; for I will forgive their iniquity, and remember their sin no more.

Reading 2: Hebrews 5:7–9

7 In the days of his flesh, Jesus offered up prayers and supplications, with loud cries and tears, to the one who was able to save him from death, and he was heard because of his reverent submission. ⁸Although he was a Son, he learned obedience through what he suffered; ⁹and having been made perfect, he became the source of eternal salvation for all who obey him.

Gospel: John 12:20–33

20 Now among those who went up to worship at the festival were some Greeks. ²¹They came to Philip, who was from Bethsaida in Galilee, and said to him, "Sir, we wish to see Jesus." ²²Philip went and told Andrew; then Andrew and Philip went and told Jesus. ²³Jesus answered them, "The hour has

come for the Son of Man to be glorified. [24]Very truly, I tell you, unless a grain of wheat falls into the earth and dies, it remains just a single grain; but if it dies, it bears much fruit. [25]Those who love their life lose it, and those who hate their life in this world will keep it for eternal life. [26]Whoever serves me must follow me, and where I am, there will my servant be also. Whoever serves me, the Father will honor.

27 "Now my soul is troubled. And what should I say— 'Father, save me from this hour'? No, it is for this reason that I have come to this hour. [28]Father, glorify your name." Then a voice came from heaven, "I have glorified it, and I will glorify it again." [29]The crowd standing there heard it and said that it was thunder. Others said, "An angel has spoken to him." [30]Jesus answered, "This voice has come for your sake, not for mine. [31] Now is the judgment of this world; now the ruler of this world will be driven out. [32]And I, when I am lifted up from the earth, will draw all people to myself." [33]He said this to indicate the kind of death he was to die.

Commentary

The Shared Testament reading from Jeremiah is a famous prophetic passage that has inspired reflection among diverse groups of Jews and Christians for centuries. Active during the political and religious crises surrounding the rise and eventual triumph of the Babylonian Empire in the sixth century B.C.E., Jeremiah in this passage looks forward to an eschatological future in which covenanted life is realized to the ultimate degree imaginable. God's people will not need to learn or pursue studies of God's Torah, because it will be internalized within their very beings. They will therefore live in perfect conformity with God's intentions. The Age to Come, a world permeated by God's justice and shalom, will have arrived.

It is essential to recognize the eschatological character of this passage. The "newness" described is not a new set of teachings that differ from the instructions written on the stone tablets of the Mosaic covenant. Rather, the newness is precisely in the way in which those teachings are conveyed. They are no longer transmitted through external media but have been divinely imprinted upon the very fabric of the human existence.

This radical newness is something that has not yet been realized among human communities. Claims over the centuries that Jeremiah's vision has been attained in this or that community are premature. It is a goal toward which God is summoning humanity.

It is within this eschatological framework that the connections between the Shared Testament and gospel readings should be explored. The passage from the Gospel of John considers the "hour" of Jesus. In this evangelist's view this is the hour of Jesus' death but also the hour of his glorification, when, after being "lifted up," Jesus draws all humanity into relationship with the Father. This phrase "lifted up" is meant to refer both to the crucifixion and to the resurrection. The dying grain of wheat brings new and eternal life into being.

Actualization

The juxtaposing of these two passages is clearly meant to associate Jeremiah's new covenant with the salvific effects of Jesus' death and resurrection. There is certainly a "newness" to the church's covenant with God in Christ. People from around the world have been drawn into a saving relationship with the God of Israel.

However, the fullness of this covenantal life with God has not yet been realized in the collective life of Christians. God's teachings have not been ingrained upon our very beings; preachers and teachers must instruct and exhort the faithful to live according to God's will. Jeremiah's vision will not be fully realized until the ultimate establishment of the reign of God, that Age to Come that Christians believe Jesus inaugurated.

The pairing of these readings, then, provides a powerful summons for the Christian community. We are reminded that the life, death, and resurrection of Jesus have drawn us into covenantal life with God. That life will one day become woven into the very chemistry of our existence, but, for now, both Jews and Christians are challenged by Jeremiah to strive for that internalization of God's will that he saw as the ultimate destiny of God's people.

E. Easter Triduum—Good Friday (Cycles A, B, C)

Reading 1: Isaiah 52:13–53:12

[13] See, my servant shall prosper;
    he shall be exalted and lifted up,
    and shall be very high.
[14] Just as there were many who were astonished at him
    —so marred was his appearance, beyond human semblance,
    and his form beyond that of mortals—
[15] so he shall startle many nations;
    kings shall shut their mouths because of him;
    for that which had not been told them they shall see,
        and that which they had not heard they shall contemplate.
53 Who has believed what we have heard?
    And to whom has the arm of the LORD been revealed?
[2] For he grew up before him like a young plant,
    and like a root out of dry ground;
    he had no form or majesty that we should look at him,
        nothing in his appearance that we should desire him.
[3] He was despised and rejected by others;
    a man of suffering and acquainted with infirmity;
    and as one from whom others hide their faces
        he was despised, and we held him of no account.
[4] Surely he has borne our infirmities
    and carried our diseases;
    yet we accounted him stricken,
        struck down by God, and afflicted.
[5] But he was wounded for our transgressions,
    crushed for our iniquities;

upon him was the punishment that made us whole,
    and by his bruises we are healed.

⁶ All we like sheep have gone astray;
    we have all turned to our own way,
and the LORD has laid on him
    the iniquity of us all.

⁷ He was oppressed, and he was afflicted,
    yet he did not open his mouth;
like a lamb that is led to the slaughter,
    and like a sheep that before its shearers is silent,
    so he did not open his mouth.

⁸ By a perversion of justice he was taken away.
    Who could have imagined his future?
For he was cut off from the land of the living,
    stricken for the transgression of my people.

⁹ They made his grave with the wicked
    and his tomb with the rich,
although he had done no violence,
    and there was no deceit in his mouth.

¹⁰ Yet it was the will of the LORD to crush him with pain.
When you make his life an offering for sin,
    he shall see his offspring, and shall prolong his days;
through him the will of the LORD shall prosper.

¹¹ Out of his anguish he shall see light;
he shall find satisfaction through his knowledge.
    The righteous one, my servant, shall make many
        righteous,
    and he shall bear their iniquities.

¹² Therefore I will allot him a portion with the great,
    and he shall divide the spoil with the strong;
because he poured out himself to death,
    and was numbered with the transgressors;
yet he bore the sin of many,
    and made intercession for the transgressors.

Reading 2: Hebrews 4:14–16; 5:7–9

14 Since, then, we have a great high priest who has passed through the heavens, Jesus, the Son of God, let us hold fast to our confession. [15]For we do not have a high priest who is unable to sympathize with our weaknesses, but we have one who in every respect has been tested as we are, yet without sin. [16]Let us therefore approach the throne of grace with boldness, so that we may receive mercy and find grace to help in time of need.

7 In the days of his flesh, Jesus offered up prayers and supplications, with loud cries and tears, to the one who was able to save him from death, and he was heard because of his reverent submission. [8]Although he was a Son, he learned obedience through what he suffered; [9]and having been made perfect, he became the source of eternal salvation for all who obey him.

Gospel: John 18:1—19:42

18 After Jesus had spoken these words, he went out with his disciples across the Kidron valley to a place where there was a garden, which he and his disciples entered. [2]Now Judas, who betrayed him, also knew the place, because Jesus often met there with his disciples. [3]So Judas brought a detachment of soldiers together with police from the chief priests and the Pharisees, and they came there with lanterns and torches and weapons. [4]Then Jesus, knowing all that was to happen to him, came forward and asked them, "Whom are you looking for?" [5]They answered, "Jesus of Nazareth." Jesus replied, "I am he." Judas, who betrayed him, was standing with them. [6]When Jesus said to them, "I am he," they stepped back and fell to the ground. [7]Again he asked them, "Whom are you looking for?" And they said, "Jesus of Nazareth." [8]Jesus answered, "I told you that I am he. So if you are looking for me, let these men go." [9]This was to fulfill the word that he had spoken, "I did not lose a single one of those whom you gave me." [10]Then Simon

Peter, who had a sword, drew it, struck the high priest's slave, and cut off his right ear. The slave's name was Malchus. [11]Jesus said to Peter, "Put your sword back into its sheath. Am I not to drink the cup that the Father has given me?"

12 So the soldiers, their officer, and the Jewish police arrested Jesus and bound him. [13]First they took him to Annas, who was the father-in-law of Caiaphas, the high priest that year. [14]Caiaphas was the one who had advised the Jews that it was better to have one person die for the people.

15 Simon Peter and another disciple followed Jesus. Since that disciple was known to the high priest, he went with Jesus into the courtyard of the high priest, [16]but Peter was standing outside at the gate. So the other disciple, who was known to the high priest, went out, spoke to the woman who guarded the gate, and brought Peter in. [17]The woman said to Peter, "You are not also one of this man's disciples, are you?" He said, "I am not." [18]Now the slaves and the police had made a charcoal fire because it was cold, and they were standing around it and warming themselves. Peter also was standing with them and warming himself.

19 Then the high priest questioned Jesus about his disciples and about his teaching. [20]Jesus answered, "I have spoken openly to the world; I have always taught in synagogues and in the temple, where all the Jews come together. I have said nothing in secret. [21]Why do you ask me? Ask those who heard what I said to them; they know what I said." [22]When he had said this, one of the police standing nearby struck Jesus on the face, saying, "Is that how you answer the high priest?" [23]Jesus answered, "If I have spoken wrongly, testify to the wrong. But if I have spoken rightly, why do you strike me?" [24]Then Annas sent him bound to Caiaphas the high priest.

25 Now Simon Peter was standing and warming himself. They asked him, "You are not also one of his disciples, are you?" He denied it and said, "I am not." [26]One of the slaves of

the high priest, a relative of the man whose ear Peter had cut off, asked, "Did I not see you in the garden with him?" ²⁷Again Peter denied it, and at that moment the cock crowed.

28 Then they took Jesus from Caiaphas to Pilate's headquarters. It was early in the morning. They themselves did not enter the headquarters, so as to avoid ritual defilement and to be able to eat the Passover. ²⁹So Pilate went out to them and said, "What accusation do you bring against this man?" ³⁰They answered, "If this man were not a criminal, we would not have handed him over to you." ³¹Pilate said to them, "Take him yourselves and judge him according to your law." The Jews replied, "We are not permitted to put anyone to death." ³²(This was to fulfill what Jesus had said when he indicated the kind of death he was to die.)

33 Then Pilate entered the headquarters again, summoned Jesus, and asked him, "Are you the King of the Jews?" ³⁴Jesus answered, "Do you ask this on your own, or did others tell you about me?" ³⁵Pilate replied, "I am not a Jew, am I? Your own nation and the chief priests have handed you over to me. What have you done?" ³⁶Jesus answered, "My kingdom is not from this world. If my kingdom were from this world, my followers would be fighting to keep me from being handed over to the Jews. But as it is, my kingdom is not from here." ³⁷Pilate asked him, "So you are a king?" Jesus answered, "You say that I am a king. For this I was born, and for this I came into the world, to testify to the truth. Everyone who belongs to the truth listens to my voice." ³⁸Pilate asked him, "What is truth?"

After he had said this, he went out to the Jews again and told them, "I find no case against him. ³⁹But you have a custom that I release someone for you at the Passover. Do you want me to release for you the King of the Jews?" ⁴⁰They shouted in reply, "Not this man, but Barabbas!" Now Barabbas was a bandit.

19 Then Pilate took Jesus and had him flogged. [2]And the soldiers wove a crown of thorns and put it on his head, and they dressed him in a purple robe. [3]They kept coming up to him, saying, "Hail, King of the Jews!" and striking him on the face. [4]Pilate went out again and said to them, "Look, I am bringing him out to you to let you know that I find no case against him." [5]So Jesus came out, wearing the crown of thorns and the purple robe. Pilate said to them, "Here is the man!" [6]When the chief priests and the police saw him, they shouted, "Crucify him! Crucify him!" Pilate said to them, "Take him yourselves and crucify him; I find no case against him." [7]The Jews answered him, "We have a law, and according to that law he ought to die because he has claimed to be the Son of God."

8 Now when Pilate heard this, he was more afraid than ever. [9]He entered his headquarters again and asked Jesus, "Where are you from?" But Jesus gave him no answer. [10]Pilate therefore said to him, "Do you refuse to speak to me? Do you not know that I have power to release you, and power to crucify you?" [11]Jesus answered him, "You would have no power over me unless it had been given you from above; therefore the one who handed me over to you is guilty of a greater sin." [12]From then on Pilate tried to release him, but the Jews cried out, "If you release this man, you are no friend of the emperor. Everyone who claims to be a king sets himself against the emperor."

13 When Pilate heard these words, he brought Jesus outside and sat on the judge's bench at a place called The Stone Pavement, or in Hebrew Gabbatha. [14]Now it was the day of Preparation for the Passover; and it was about noon. He said to the Jews, "Here is your King!" [15]They cried out, "Away with him! Away with him! Crucify him!" Pilate asked them, "Shall I crucify your King?" The chief priests answered, "We have no king but the emperor." [16]Then he handed him over to them to be crucified.

So they took Jesus; [17]and carrying the cross by himself, he went out to what is called The Place of the Skull, which in Hebrew is called Golgotha. [18]There they crucified him, and with him two others, one on either side, with Jesus between them. [19]Pilate also had an inscription written and put on the cross. It read, "Jesus of Nazareth, the King of the Jews." [20]Many of the Jews read this inscription, because the place where Jesus was crucified was near the city; and it was written in Hebrew, in Latin, and in Greek. [21]Then the chief priests of the Jews said to Pilate, "Do not write, 'The King of the Jews,' but, 'This man said, I am King of the Jews.'" [22]Pilate answered, "What I have written I have written." [23]When the soldiers had crucified Jesus, they took his clothes and divided them into four parts, one for each soldier. They also took his tunic; now the tunic was seamless, woven in one piece from the top. [24]So they said to one another, "Let us not tear it, but cast lots for it to see who will get it." This was to fulfill what the scripture says,

"They divided my clothes among themselves,
and for my clothing they cast lots."

25 And that is what the soldiers did.

Meanwhile, standing near the cross of Jesus were his mother, and his mother's sister, Mary the wife of Clopas, and Mary Magdalene. [26]When Jesus saw his mother and the disciple whom he loved standing beside her, he said to his mother, "Woman, here is your son." [27]Then he said to the disciple, "Here is your mother." And from that hour the disciple took her into his own home.

28 After this, when Jesus knew that all was now finished, he said (in order to fulfill the scripture), "I am thirsty." [29]A jar full of sour wine was standing there. So they put a sponge full of the wine on a branch of hyssop and held it to his mouth. [30]When Jesus had received the wine, he said, "It is finished." Then he bowed his head and gave up his spirit.

31 Since it was the day of Preparation, the Jews did not want the bodies left on the cross during the sabbath, especially because that sabbath was a day of great solemnity. So they asked Pilate to have the legs of the crucified men broken and the bodies removed. [32]Then the soldiers came and broke the legs of the first and of the other who had been crucified with him. [33]But when they came to Jesus and saw that he was already dead, they did not break his legs. [34]Instead, one of the soldiers pierced his side with a spear, and at once blood and water came out. [35](He who saw this has testified so that you also may believe. His testimony is true, and he knows that he tells the truth.) [36]These things occurred so that the scripture might be fulfilled, "None of his bones shall be broken." [37]And again another passage of scripture says, "They will look on the one whom they have pierced."

38 After these things, Joseph of Arimathea, who was a disciple of Jesus, though a secret one because of his fear of the Jews, asked Pilate to let him take away the body of Jesus. Pilate gave him permission; so he came and removed his body. [39]Nicodemus, who had at first come to Jesus by night, also came, bringing a mixture of myrrh and aloes, weighing about a hundred pounds. [40]They took the body of Jesus and wrapped it with the spices in linen cloths, according to the burial custom of the Jews. [41]Now there was a garden in the place where he was crucified, and in the garden there was a new tomb in which no one had ever been laid. [42]And so, because it was the Jewish day of Preparation, and the tomb was nearby, they laid Jesus there.

Commentary

The Shared Testament reading for Good Friday presents the lengthiest of the four Suffering Servant songs that are found in the writings of Isaiah of the Exile, also known as

Deutero- or Second-Isaiah. Composed in the context of the exile of the Judean aristocracy to Babylon in the sixth century B.C.E., the songs have produced much discussion over the centuries regarding the identity of the Suffering Servant. Because of the poetic nature of these texts, a variety of possible identifications are defensible.

Some have suggested that the servant is a collective figure for the entire people of Israel. He thus symbolizes Israel's past, its present crisis of the Exile, and points toward an ideal Israel in the future. Some identify the servant as an individual person—as the prophet Isaiah of the Exile himself; as one of his disciples; as the exiled Judean king, Jehoiachin; or as some other historical personage. Others see the servant as more of a fictitious symbolic individual representing either Israel's sinfulness in the past or its ideal faithfulness in the future.

It is probably best to avoid trying to limit the identity of the servant to only one of these options. Given the poetical quality of these songs, the figure of the servant blends collective and individual qualities and transcends past, present, and future. He both personifies Israel's story and through his personal experiences affects the future of the entire people.

It is useful to relate the Suffering Servant songs to the overall theology of Isaiah of the Exile. This prophet in the Isaian tradition understood that the Exile was the result of Israel's infidelity to its covenant with God (e.g., Isa 42:24–25), but also saw that God would liberate the exiles. In a new Exodus, they would soon be able to return to Judah (e.g., Isa 43:14–21). "In the LORD all the offspring of Israel shall triumph and glory" (45:25). This unexpected and amazing development, Deutero-Isaiah believed, would startle the Gentile nations into a recognition of the supremacy and power of the God of Israel (e.g., Isa 49:22–26).

In this process the servant was to play an important role (e.g., 49:1–7). Although afflicted and judged to be "struck down by God" (53:4), "cut off from the land of the living" (53:8), the servant's sufferings were actually "an offering for sin" (53:10), and thus he would experience restoration and "see his offspring" (53:10). This Suffering Servant "shall prosper, shall be exalted and lifted up" (52:13) and "so he shall startle many nations" and silence kings (52:15). "It is too little a thing that you should be my servant to raise up the tribes of Jacob and to restore the survivors of Israel; I will give you as a light to the nations, that my salvation may reach to the ends of the earth" (49:6).

In other words, the prophet perceived that God could use the tragedy of Israel's exile to bring about unexpected good. Indeed, Israel had suffered even more that its sins deserved (40:2), but this humiliation would result in the acknowledgment of God's sovereignty by the pagan peoples when they witnessed how the God of Israel restored the suffering Israel of God. The prophet had the mission to proclaim this, to encourage the exiles to return home when their chance came, because "kings shall see and stand up, princes, and they shall prostrate themselves, because of the LORD, who is faithful, the Holy One of Israel, who has chosen you" (49:7).

It is easy to imagine why this Isaian passage proved to be powerfully attractive to the earliest followers of Jesus. Like the exiles in Babylon, they had to cope with tragedy—the death by torture of a righteous servant of God. Even in the aftermath of their experience of the Crucified One raised to transcendent glory, they probably wondered, "Why this senseless death? Why should such horrifying atrocity occur?"

In wrestling with such profound questions, Isaiah of the Exile provided Jesus' disciples with needed insights and helpful answers. They realized that their thoughts should not fixate on the reasons for terrible evil but rather on God's ability to bring tremendous good out of it. Jesus was thus seen as the Suffering Servant par excellence. Although his torments made him appear as a failure and rejected by God, God raised him on high. He thus became a "Light to the Nations," as evidenced in the early church by the growing mission to the Gentiles.

Actualization

This christological application of the Isaian Suffering Servant songs is undoubtedly the reason for matching his fourth song with the Johannine passion narrative on Good Friday. This gospel text has its own intrinsic difficulties in terms of Jewish-Christian relations, most notably in its recurrent use of the phrase "the Jews" and the way in which Pilate interacts with them to bring about Jesus' execution.[8] The comments here are restricted to how the gospel lection can be brought into relationship with the Shared Testament reading from Isaiah. Indeed, focusing on this relationship is one strategy for coping with the anti-Jewish polemical aspects of the gospel.

An overarching theological point of these readings is that God says "no!" to the ultimate triumph of evil. Covenantal life with God includes within it a recurrent theme of disaster and suffering caused by evil, but it is countered by a divine restoration that brings unanticipated blessings. Evil does not exist so that God can bring goodness out of it, but evil, ultimately, does not have the final word because God is supreme.

Thus, the Babylonian Exile, even if partially self-inflicted, was not the end of the covenantal life between God and Israel. God restored the exiles and thereby reaffirmed their mission to be a Light to the Nations. The crucifixion of Jesus was not the end of his covenantal life with his Abba. Christians perceive that God exalted Jesus to glorious life and thereby implemented the divine mandate to be Light to the Nations in an unexpectedly powerful manner.

It is important to observe that this pattern of tragedy and restoration did not come to an end with the Resurrection. Such a conclusion would be inevitable if one wrongly understood Isaiah to be predicting only the suffering service of Christ. However, if Isaiah is comprehended as inspired with insight into a pattern of God's actions in human history, which Christians, to be sure, see manifest to the ultimate degree in the story of Jesus, then God's ability to bring goodness out of evil is something that continues in the lives of people today. Some modern Jews and Christians, for example, in pondering the atrocity of the Holocaust, see an Isaian pattern of disaster and restoration in the reestablishment of a Jewish state in 1948.

The pastoral implications of respecting Second Isaiah on his own terms are enormous. Christian congregations can be invited to reflect on the death and resurrection experiences in their own lives. They can be encouraged to look beyond the immediacy of pain and suffering to the possibilities for renewal or strengthening that, with time, can sometimes occur. They can be summoned to ponder the majesty of a God who can even work through people's sinfulness to continue to summon humanity into a freely given commitment to God's designs for our future.

NOTES

1. Pontifical Biblical Commission, "The Interpretation of the Bible in the Church," *Origins* 23/29 (January 26, 1994), IV, A, 3.

2. Raymond E. Brown, *The Gospel According to John: I-XII*, The Anchor Bible 29 (New York: Doubleday, 1966), 523.

3. See, e.g., Robert B. Coote, *In Defense of Revolution: The Elohist History* (Minneapolis, Minn.: Fortress, 1991).

4. See the insightful study by Jon D. Levenson, *The Death and Resurrection of the Beloved Son: The Transformation of Child Sacrifice in Judaism and Christianity* (New Haven, Conn.: Yale University Press, 1993), esp. 3–17, 111–14.

5. Ibid., 138.

6. Coote, *In Defense of Revolution*, 77–90.

7. Shalom Spiegel, *The Last Trial—The Akedah: On the Legends and Lore of the Command to Abraham to Offer Isaac as a Sacrifice*, reprint ed. (Woodstock, Vt: Jewish Lights Publishing, 1993).

8. These matters are addressed in the volume on John's gospel in this series prepared by George M. Smiga. See also his *Pain and Polemic: Anti-Judaism in the Gospels* (Mahwah, N.J.: Paulist Press, A Stimulus Book, 1992). At the 2000 and 2001 annual meetings of the Catholic Biblical Association of America, the issue of "the Jews" in the Johannine passion narrative was studied in great detail by the Continuing Seminar on Biblical Issues in Jewish-Christian Relations. The Seminar's deliberations produced a suggested revised lection for future use whenever the lectionary is updated. See Philip A. Cunningham, "Translating and Excerpting the Johannine Passion Narrative for Liturgical Proclamation," *The SIDIC Review*, 34/3 and 35/1 (2001–2002): 8–18.

AFTERWORD

The Pontifical Biblical Commission's 2001 Study: The Jewish People and Their Sacred Scriptures in the Christian Bible

The five sets of sample lectionary readings just explored were selected in order to illustrate the various strategies that can be used in setting free the unfathomable riches of the Shared Testament. Depending on the passage in question, different techniques need to be employed to bring out the multiple meanings and to relate them to the Christian Testament readings. Treatments of Jeremiah's "new covenant" prophecy, for example, must highlight its essentially eschatological character in order to understand it properly as well as to comprehend accurately its implications for the Christian gospel. Likewise, the historical setting of Isaiah of Jerusalem's Emmanuel sign to King Ahaz must be understood if the theological genius of Matthew is to be fully appreciated. In some ways the exemplar passages treated above represent some of the more vivid and famous juxtapositions of Shared Testament and Christian Testament lections. Preachers and teachers, however, should try to utilize the principles described in the preface and modeled in the sample passages for *all* of the liturgical readings throughout the three-year Sunday lectionary cycle.

Many of these principles also appear in a new study from the Pontifical Biblical Commission that was released as this volume was being prepared for publication. Entitled *The Jewish People and Their Sacred Scriptures in the Christian Bible*, about three-fourths of the roughly two-hundred-page study is devoted to the relationship between the Jewish Bible and the New Testament.

Although the commission prefers to retain the traditional language of "Old Testament," it clearly does not espouse the equally traditional Christian supersessionist reading of these sacred texts:

> The Old Testament in itself has great value as the Word of God. To read the Old Testament as Christians then does not mean wishing to find everywhere direct reference to Jesus and to Christian realities. True, for Christians, all the Old Testament economy is in movement towards Christ; if then the Old Testament is read in the light of Christ, one can, retrospectively, perceive something of this movement.[1]

The commission's characterization of christological readings as "retrospective" is important for a number of reasons. First, it disallows the standard Christian accusation that Jews are blind for not seeing the (allegedly) obvious presence of Christ in their own scriptures. For the commission, "this is a retrospective perception whose point of departure is not in the text as such, but in the events of the New Testament proclaimed by the apostolic preaching. It cannot be said, therefore, that Jews do not see what has been proclaimed in the text, but that the Christian, in the light of Christ and in the Spirit, discovers in the text an additional meaning that was hidden there.[2]

Second, if the Christian reading of the Shared Testament is a valid retrospective one, then rabbinic retrospective interpretations of the Torah, the Prophets, and the Writings must also be legitimate. As the commission puts it:

> Christians can and ought to admit that the Jewish reading of the Bible is a possible one, in continuity with the Jewish Sacred Scriptures from the Second Temple period, a reading analogous to the Christian reading which developed in parallel fashion. Each of these two readings is a part of the vision of

each respective faith of which it is a product and an expression. Consequently, they cannot be reduced one into the other.[3]

Third, if the rabbinic tradition developed in parallel and analogous fashion to Christian traditions of biblical interpretation, then it follows, as has been declared in earlier documents, that Christians can learn more about God by reading rabbinic texts. "Christians can…learn much from Jewish exegesis practiced for more than two thousand years, and, in fact, they have learned much in the course of history."[4]

The Jewish People and Their Sacred Scriptures in the Christian Bible also speaks about the Hebrew prophets in ways that should guide Christian preaching and teaching of prophetic texts. To my knowledge, it is the first Roman Catholic document to discuss the biblical prophets in such depth and with such sensitivity to the implications for Christian-Jewish relations:

> It would be wrong to consider the prophecies of the Old Testament as some kind of photographic anticipations of future events. All the texts, including those which later were read as messianic prophecies, already had an immediate import and meaning for their contemporaries before attaining a fuller meaning for future hearers.…The original task of the prophet was to help his contemporaries understand the events and the times they lived in from God's viewpoint. Accordingly, excessive insistence, characteristic of a certain apologetic, on the probative value attributable to the fulfillment of prophecy must be discarded. This insistence has contributed to harsh judgments by Christians of Jews and their reading of the Old Testament: the more reference to Christ is found in Old Testament texts, the more the incredulity of the Jews is considered inexcusable and obstinate.[5]

These comments reinforce what was said earlier in this volume about lectionary preaching, particularly during the Advent season. The Hebrew prophets cannot be portrayed as fortunetellers. If preachers and teachers fail to convey in their sermons and lessons that the church's application of the Hebrew biblical prophecies to Christ are retrospective, then they unwittingly dispose their congregations to think of Jews as closed-minded or faithless.

Finally, the study has noteworthy things to say about eschatology. After observing that Christian hopes for the ultimate salvation of the world are "already substantially realized in the mystery of Christ," the commission explains that "what has already been accomplished in Christ must yet be accomplished in us and in the world. The definitive fulfillment will be at the end with the resurrection of the dead, a new heaven and a new earth."[6]

This statement reiterates similar comments made in 1985 by the Vatican Commission for Religious Relations with the Jews.[7] However, here the Pontifical Biblical Commission goes on to consider the eschaton itself: "Jewish messianic expectation is not in vain. It can become for us Christians a powerful stimulant to keep alive the eschatological [i.e., unfinished] dimension of our faith. Like them, we too live in expectation. The difference is that for us the One who is to come will have the traits of the Jesus who has already come and is already present and active among us."[8]

The explicit declaration that "Jewish messianic expectation is not in vain" is an important one, but it is overshadowed by the phrase "the traits of the Jesus who has already come." Clearly, these "traits" are not merely physical or the commission could have simply stated that "the One who is to come will be the Jesus who has already come." This raises interesting possibilities for future theological research and dialogue. For instance, for Christians "traits" must refer to the Crucified and

Raised One who brings the church into covenant with God. Israel, also in covenant with God, has in the gift of the Torah, in the words of the commission, "a manifestation of the all-wise divine will."[9] Would it not follow then if Jewish expectations for the eschaton are "not in vain," that for Jews "traits" of that divine Will shall also be recognizable at the eschaton?

Be that as it may, the commission's eschatological reflections have immediate relevance for Christian preaching and teaching on prophetic eschatological texts such as Jeremiah 31:31ff. or Isaiah 2:1ff. While for the church such hopes are "already substantially realized in the mystery of Christ," they have not been fully accomplished. Teachers and preachers would do well to remind their listeners that Jews and Christians both wait for the ultimate fulfillment of God's intentions for us.

By utilizing the appropriate methods outlined in this volume as determined by the readings themselves, preachers and teachers can help acquaint Christians with the largely unknown and perennially revealing spiritual treasures of the Shared Testament. They will also deepen the faithful's understanding of the Christian Testament. In doing so, Christian leaders will not be expressing only the modern church's esteem for the Jewish people and tradition. They will also be respecting the historical and literary character, the incarnate quality, of the Sacred Scripture itself, in which "the words of God, expressed in human language, are in every way like human speech, just as the Word of the eternal father, when he took on himself the weak flesh of human beings, became like them."

NOTES

1. Pontifical Biblical Commission, *The Jewish People and Their Sacred Scriptures in the Christian Bible* (Vatican City: Libreria Editrice Vaticana, 2002), III, A, 6.

2. Ibid.

3. Ibid., II, A, 7. My thanks to Laurence Frizzel for pointing out some translation issues from the French original.

4. Ibid.

5. Ibid., II, A, 5.

6. Ibid.

7. Vatican Commission for Religious Relations with the Jews, "Notes on the Correct Way to Present the Jews and Judaism in Preaching and Catechesis in the Roman Catholic Church," II, 6–11, *Origins* 15/7 (July 4, 1985).

8. Pontifical Biblical Commission, *The Jewish People and Their Sacred Scriptures in the Christian Bible*, II, A, 5.

9. Ibid., II, B, 6.

10. *Dei Verbum*, 13, in Vatican Council II, *The Basic Sixteen Documents: Constitutions, Decrees, Declarations*, ed. Austin Flannery (New York: Costello Publishing, 1996).

QUESTIONS FOR REFLECTION AND DISCUSSION

1. In recent years there has been a movement to incorporate religious education into the liturgical life of the community and to structure curricula around the lectionary. According to the Preface to this volume, what are some implications of this move for Christian-Jewish relations? What steps can preachers and educators take to ensure that education based on the lectionary promotes accurate understandings of Jews and Judaism?

2. One of the important aspects of the lectionary's use of the Shared Testament is the attitudes toward the Hebrew tradition that it might engender. Imagine that you are instructing people preparing for initiation into the church through the Rite of Christian Initiation of Adults or a similar formative process. How would you explain the process of rereading by which the ancient texts of Israel were interpreted in new ways by the followers of the Risen Jesus? Could you do this in ways that preserve the validity of other traditions of understanding those texts, such as the rabbinic heritage?

3. Select a familiar prophetic reading that is not discussed in this book. Using the perspectives described in the Preface and expressed by the Pontifical Biblical Commission in the Afterword, how would you preach or teach this passage to promote a fuller appreciation of the nature of biblical prophecy?

4. The lectionary excerpts only a tiny fraction of the inexhaustible wealth of the Shared Testament. What

could preachers and teachers do to encourage a wider familiarity with the inspired texts of ancient Israel among Christian congregations? Suppose that the time has come for the next revision of the lectionary used in your church or denomination. You have been invited to submit suggestions on how scriptural passages should be selected. What recommendations would you make based on the concerns of this volume of The Word Set Free?

SELECT BIBLIOGRAPHY

1. General Resources on the Bible

Achtemeier, Paul J., gen. ed. *Harper's Bible Dictionary*. Harper & Row, 1985.

Alter, Robert, and Frank Kermode, eds. *The Literary Guide to the Bible*. Harvard University Press, 1987.

Boadt, Lawrence. *Reading the Old Testament: An Introduction*. Paulist Press, 1984.

Brown, Raymond E., Joseph A. Fitzmyer, and Roland E. Murphy, eds. *The New Jerome Biblical Commentary*. Prentice-Hall, 1990.

Buttrick, George Arthur, dictionary ed. *The Interpreter's Dictionary of the Bible*, 4 vols. and supp. Abingdon, 1962, 1976.

Coote, Robert B., and Mary P. Coote. *Power, Politics, and the Making of the Bible: An Introduction*. Fortress, 1990.

Freedman, David Noel, editor-in-chief. *The Anchor Bible Dictionary*, 6 vols. Doubleday, 1992.

Gottwald, Norman K. *The Hebrew Bible: A Socio-Literary Introduction*. Fortress, 1985.

May, James L., gen. ed. *Harper's Bible Commentary*. Harper & Row, 1988.

2. The Lectionary and Jewish-Christian Relations

Beck, Norman A. *Mature Christianity in the Twenty-First Century.* Crossroad, 1994.

Bishops' Committee on the Liturgy, National Conference of Catholic Bishops. *God's Mercy Endures Forever: Guidelines on the Presentation of Jews and Judaism in Catholic Preaching.* U.S.C.C., 1988.

Cunningham, Philip A. *Proclaiming Shalom: Lectionary Introductions to Foster the Catholic and Jewish Relationship.* Liturgical Press, 1995.

Pawlikowski, John T., and James A. Wilde. *When Catholics Speak About Jews.* Liturgy Training Pub., 1987.

Williamson, Clark M., and Ronald J. Allen. *Interpreting Difficult Texts: Anti-Judaism and Christian Preaching.* Trinity, 1989.

KEYWORDS

Actualization	the process of constructing the meaning and implications of a biblical text for communities of faith today.
Aqedah, akedah	"the binding," the traditional Jewish way of referring to the events of Genesis 22:1–18.
Christian Testament	the second part of the Christian Bible, which is the witness to the importance of Jesus Christ by the apostolic generations of the church.
Eschaton, eschatological	concepts related to the end-times, the final destiny of all creation when it is fully in accord with God's designs. Some theologies stress a "realized eschatology" and what has already been accomplished in the achievement of God's intentions. Others stress a "futurist eschatology" and what yet remains to be fulfilled.
Polemic, polemical	texts that are argumentative and make derogatory suggestions or exaggerations about opponents of the author.

Prophecy   speaking on behalf of God. While proclaiming God's will to their contemporaries, biblical prophets occasionally refer to the future, but usually in an eschatological way. Biblical prophecy should be distinguished from colloquial uses of the term which reduce prophecy to predicting detail of future events.

Rereadings   instances of later biblical writers actualizing earlier biblical texts for their own contemporaries.

Shared Testament   the first part of the Christian Bible, those scriptures of ancient Israel that are considered to be of canonical authority by the church.

Supersessionism   the theological assertion that the church has superseded or replaced Jews as the chosen people of God because of Jewish responsibility for the death of Jesus. Although now discredited by the church, it was the dominant Christian view of Judaism for eighteen hundred years.

Leon Klenicki, editor, *Toward A Theological Encounter* (A Stimulus Book, 1991).

David Burrell and Yehezkel Landau, editors, *Voices from Jerusalem* (A Stimulus Book, 1991).

John Rousmaniere, *A Bridge to Dialogue: The Story of Jewish-Christian Relations,* edited by James A. Carpenter and Leon Klenicki (A Stimulus Book, 1991).

Michael E. Lodahl, *Shekhinah/Spirit* (A Stimulus Book, 1992).

George M. Smiga, *Pain and Polemic: Anti-Judaism in the Gospels* (A Stimulus Book, 1992).

Eugene J. Fisher, editor, *Interwoven Destinies: Jews and Christians Through the Ages* (A Stimulus Book, 1993).

Anthony Kenny, *Catholics, Jews and the State of Israel* (A Stimulus Book, 1993).

Eugene J. Fisher, editor, *Visions of the Other: Jewish and Christian Theologians Assess the Dialogue* (A Stimulus Book, 1995).

Leon Klenicki and Geoffrey Wigoder, editors, *A Dictionary of the Jewish-Christian Dialogue* (Expanded Edition), (A Stimulus Book, 1995).

Philip A. Cunningham and Arthur F. Starr, eds., *Sharing Shalom: A Process for Local Interfaith Dialogue Between Christians and Jews* (A Stimulus Book, 1998).

Frank E. Eakin, Jr., *What Price Prejudice?: Christian Antisemitism in America* (A Stimulus Book, 1998).

Ekkehard Schuster & Reinhold Boschert-Kimmig, *Hope Against Hope: Johann Baptist Metz and Elie Wiesel Speak Out on the Holocaust* (A Stimulus Book, 1999).

Mary C. Boys, *Has God Only One Blessing?: Judaism as a Source of Christian Understanding* (A Stimulus Book, 2000).

Peter Wortsman, editor, *Recommendation Whether to Confiscate, Destroy and Burn All Jewish Books: A Classic Treatise against Anti-Semitism* by Johannes Reuchlin (A Stimulus Book, 2000).

Avery Dulles, S.J. and Leon Klenicki, editors, *The Holocaust, Never to Be Forgotten: Reflections on the Holy See's Document* We Remember (A Stimulus Book, 2000).

Philip A. Cunningham, *A Story of Shalom: The Calling of Christians and Jews by a Covenanting God* (A Stimulus Book, 2001).

STIMULUS BOOKS are developed by Stimulus Foundation, a not-for-profit organization, and are published by Paulist Press. The Foundation wishes to further the publication of scholarly books on Jewish and Christian topics that are of importance to Judaism and Christianity.

Stimulus Foundation was established by an erstwhile refugee from Nazi Germany who intends to contribute with these publications to the improvement of communication between Jews and Christians.

Books for publication in this Series will be selected by a committee of the Foundation, and offers of manuscripts and works in progress should be addressed to:

Stimulus Foundation
c/o Paulist Press
997 Macarthur Boulevard
Mahwah, N.J. 07430
www.paulistpress.com